WELL WRITTEN AND DOCUMENTED, this book exposes the dangers of Freemasonry. This secret society is actually a false religion, claiming to offer "Divine Light" but in fact deceiving and leading astray many through its counterfeit Christianity. Jesus warned, "Make sure that the light you think you have is not actually darkness" (Luke 11:35, NLT). Dr. Hinnant cuts through all of Freemasonry's confusing speech, gets to the core of every lie and deception, and presents the corrective biblical truth in a clear, comprehensive manner. Freemasonry lures the naïve away from salvation through Christ alone, claiming instead salvation comes through good works. The reader is left with a clear choice: you can be a Freemason or a Christian but not both, as the two faiths are mutually exclusive. A definite must-read for current Masons, anyone considering membership, and all seekers of truth desiring to deepen their understanding of secret societies like Freemasonry.

Dr. Marsha Scudder Rano, D.Min., D.Th.
ParacleteProTruth, Marsha Rano Ministries, President

FREEMASONRY:
AN EXPOSÉ!

FREEMASONRY: AN EXPOSÉ!

SHINING LIGHT ON FREEMASONRY'S DARK TEACHINGS

GREG HINNANT

Freemasonry: An Exposé!
Copyright © 2024 by Greg Hinnant
First edition
Printed in the United States of America
ISBN: 978-1-964359-08-3
E-book ISBN: 978-1-964359-10-6
LCCN: 2024925001

All rights reserved. This book or parts thereof may not be reproduced in any form, stored in a retrieval system, or transmitted in any form by any means—electronic, mechanical, photocopy, recording, or otherwise—without prior written permission of the author, except as provided by United States of America copyright law.

Unless otherwise noted, all Scripture quotations are from *The New Scofield Reference Bible*, King James Version (New York: Oxford University Press, 1967). *The New Scofield Reference Bible* contains introductions, annotations, subject chain references, and some word changes in the King James Version that will help the reader. Scripture quotations marked CJB are from the *Complete Jewish Bible*, Copyright 1998 and 2016 by David. H. Stern. Used by permission. All rights reserved worldwide.

Scripture quotations marked ESV are from the Holy Bible, English Standard Version. Copyright © 2001 by Crossway Bibles, a division of Good News Publishers. Used by permission.

Scripture quotations marked KJV are from the King James Version of the Bible. Public domain.

Scripture quotations marked NAS are from the New American Standard Bible, copyright © 1960, 1962, 1963, 1968, 1971, 1972, 1973, 1975, 1977, 1995 by The Lockman Foundation. Used by permission. (www.Lockman.org)

Scripture quotations marked NCV are taken from the New Century Version®. Copyright © 2005 by Thomas Nelson. Used by permission. All rights reserved.

Scripture quotations marked NIV are taken from the Holy Bible, New International Version®, niv®. Copyright © 1973, 1978, 1984, 2011 by Biblica, Inc.™ Used by permission of Zondervan. All rights reserved worldwide. www.zondervan.com. The "NIV" and "New International Version" are trademarks registered in the United States Patent and Trademark Office by Biblica, Inc.™

Scripture quotations marked NKJV are taken from the New King James Version®. Copyright © 1982 by Thomas Nelson. Used by permission. All rights reserved.

Scripture quotations marked NLT are from the Holy Bible, New Living Translation, copyright © 1996, 2004, 2007. Used by permission of Tyndale House Publishers, Inc., Wheaton, IL 60189.

All rights reserved.

AUTHOR'S NOTE: Some Scripture quotations have specific words and/or phrases that I am emphasizing. I have added italics to these verses to show that emphasis. Also, in some of the Scripture quotations, I have inserted in brackets explanatory text to help with the understanding of certain words and phrases.

Address all personal correspondence to:
Greg Hinnant
www.greghinnantministries.org

Cover design by Elizabeth Shreve

Individuals and church groups may order books directly from Greg Hinnant Ministries, Amazon, the publisher and many other online retail locations. Refer to the Deeper Revelation Books website for distribution information, as well as an online catalog of all our books.

Published by: **Deeper Revelation Books**
Revealing "the deep things of God" (1 Cor. 2:10)
P.O. Box 4260
Cleveland, TN 37320 423-478-2843
Website: www.deeperrevelationbooks.org
Email: info@deeperrevelationbooks.org

Deeper Revelation Books assists Christian authors in publishing and distributing their books. Final responsibility for design, content, permissions, editorial accuracy, and doctrinal views, either expressed or implied, belongs to the author.

*To the liberation
of spiritual captives everywhere ...*

CONTENTS

Introduction 17

Chapter One
LOOKING BACK: HISTORICAL PERSPECTIVES 21

Chapter Two
LOOKING IN: EXAMINING FREEMASONRY'S
WORKING PARTS 31

Chapter Three
LOOKING DEEPER: EXAMINING FREEMASONRY'S
CORE HERESIES 49

Chapter Four
LOOKING THROUGH: PENETRATING FREEMASONRY'S
FAÇADE 99

Chapter Five
LOOKING FORWARD: OUR COURSE OF ACTION 115

Appendix
MORGAN, FINNEY, AND REVIVAL 129

Bibliography 135

Other Books by the Author 141

About the Author 143

INTRODUCTION

A SECRETIVE SOCIETY with secret handshakes, passwords, signs, rituals, oaths, teachings, meetings, and other hidden things—this sounds like a strange, esoteric, non-Christian, cultish sect, doesn't it? Well, read on.

Our subject is Freemasonry. What began as a research paper for a friend's website turned quickly into a book. My research has been conducted with an open mind and I write this review with dispassionate solemnity. No Mason has wronged or offended me. Determined not to draw conclusions before adequately researching the subject, I have done my homework, patiently and thoroughly. Three facts support this.

First, I have personal, albeit limited, experience in the subject. In high school, I was a member of DeMolay, the Masonic organization for young men. There I witnessed introductory level Masonic places and practices: the Masonic temple,[1] secret handshakes, passwords, closed meetings, the Masonic altar, its Bible, DeMolay lectures (the Flower Talk), and so forth. Our chapter even visited the North Carolina Grand Masonic Lodge and put on a play about the tragic history of DeMolay's namesake, Jacques de Molay. The last Grand Master of the Knights Templars, Molay died a martyr in 1314 rather than divulge the names of his fellow Templars to their persecutors. My paternal uncle, father-in-law,

---

1. While Freemasons sometimes refer to their temples as lodges, strictly speaking, "lodge" refers to the gathering of Masons, "temple" to the buildings in which they gather.

and grandfather-in-law were Masons, the latter being Grand Master of the Grand Masonic Lodge of North Carolina and a Shriner. And finally, I attended a Masonic relative's funeral recently, where I witnessed firsthand the carefully rehearsed, elaborate Masonic burial rituals, complete with a verbose oration, pine branches, lambskin aprons, white gloves, choreographed hand motions, and verbal chants repeated with sadly misguided devotion.

Second, I consulted Masonic authorities. Specifically, I interviewed an experienced Freemason lecturer here in North Carolina and a knowledgeable executive at America's oldest Masonic publisher. Both men—yes, you guessed it—asked me *not* to disclose their names! So, I have obliged them.

Third, I reviewed authoritative Masonic works. I closely examined the very informative, extensive introductory material in two Masonic Bibles, the smaller *The Holy Bible, Master Mason Edition*,[2] and the much larger *The Holy Bible, Heirloom Family Edition*,[3] in which the

---

2. *The Holy Bible, Master Mason Edition*, (Wichita, KS; Heirloom Bible Publishers), 1991. This smaller Bible contains: a description of the progressive steps (degrees) in Masonry, excerpted from Albert Pike's *Morals and Dogmas*; a description of the progressive steps (degrees) in York Rite Masonry, again using Pike's text; and questions and answers relating to character, places, words and phrases used in Masonic symbolism.

3. *The Holy Bible, Heirloom Family Edition*, (Wichita, KS; Heirloom Bible Publishers), 1988. This much larger Bible, typical of those usually found on Masonic altars, contains the following information compiled by C. H. Stauffacher: the internal workings (degrees) of Freemasonry; the degrees of Scottish Rite Masonry; the Order of The Eastern Star; and questions and answers relating to the history and work of Freemasonry and Eastern Star.

bulk of Masonic degree instruction may be found. The unexamined remainder of these Bibles is the standard Authorized (KJV) Version of the Bible. I purchased the famous, massive *Morals and Dogma*, authored by the nineteenth-century prodigious Masonic thinker, Albert Pike, in which he set forth with typical Masonic loquaciousness his well-respected Masonic philosophical and religious doctrine. Most importantly, I carefully perused arguably the most significant Masonic book, *The Builders*, authored by the minister, distinguished scholar, and Masonic authority, Joseph Ford Newton. Also, I visited numerous excellent, informative Masonic websites, reading pages on everything from Freemasonry's history to its philosophy to its current practices to its apologetics, including its rhythmically repeated claims that it is *not* a secret society, religion, or threat to the church. Finally, I have interpreted extracts from these sources with careful contextual integrity. I don't appreciate my statements being taken out of context, so I have endeavored not to do so to my Masonic sources.

There are other facts you should know. Freemasonry has been condemned by the Roman Catholic Church for almost 300 years. Catholics who join are held to be "in a state of grave [deadly, damning] sin, and may not receive Holy Communion."[4] Many Protestant denominations have also officially identified Freemasonry as a heretical organization.[5]

---

4. "From 1738 to 1983" Catholics joining or supporting Freemasonry "were censured with automatic excommunication." See "Papal Ban of Freemasonry": https://en.wikipedia.org/wiki/Papal_ban_of_Freemasonry (accessed 7/9/2024).

5. At least twenty Protestant denominations, including the Southern

Finally, everything I share about Freemasonry[6] is also true of Shriners, since all Shriners are Masons. It is furthermore true of Eastern Star (women and men), Rainbow (girls), and DeMolay, since these associate organizations stand on the foundational beliefs of Freemasonry and, though unrealized, under its dark spiritual covering.

This is my first foray into the field of Polemic Theology. For years my writings have focused on Old and New Testament Biblical Studies, Christian Living, Devotional works, and Eschatology. I write this book for two simple reasons. First, many Christians are entangled in Freemasonry's dark, deceptive web. By no means do I wish to deride Masons, but by every means I intend to liberate Christians embracing their heresies and spare others from becoming Masons. Second, this book partially fulfills my general ministerial duty to "earnestly contend for the faith" (Jude 3) by earnestly contending against these heresies.

So, let us begin uncovering very revealing facts about Freemasonry's very concealed Craft. We will look back, look in, look deeper, look through and, finally, look forward, offering biblical recommendations for action.

—Greg Hinnant

Baptist Convention, acknowledge the heretical nature of Freemasonry's teachings, though not all require its members to leave the lodge. See: Field, Eddy D. II, Field, Eddy D. III, "Freemasonry and The Christian," 143, see: https://tms.edu/wp-content/uploads/2021/09/tmsj5g.pdf (accessed 7/30/2024).

6. "Freemasonry" and "Masonry" are universally used interchangeably.

Chapter One

LOOKING BACK: HISTORICAL PERSPECTIVES

To understand any subject or entity, we must first understand its origins. So, we will begin our examination of Freemasonry by giving some key historical perspectives. Freemasonry was rooted in secrecy centuries ago, claims links to the ancient mystery religions, and purports to possess secret wisdom. Let's examine these origins more closely.

Freemasonry: Rooted in Secrecy

Freemasonry began innocently enough, as a trade guild comprised of stonemasons employed building the great cathedrals of Europe during Medieval times. These original operative[1] Masons banded together to keep their craft's secrets to themselves, thus ensuring their specialized services would be needed whenever the (Roman Catholic) church built or repaired its massive, spired, stone houses of worship. Since they were skilled laborers in high demand, and thus able to move about Medieval Europe freely when most people were bound by feudal service, these operative masons became

---

1. "Operative" Masons (were) are practicing stone workers and artisans; "speculative" Masons are members of the modern Masonic lodge having other trades or professions.

known as "free" Masons.

As cathedral construction slowed, the demand for skilled stonemasons decreased, as did the members in operative Masons' secret societies. To maintain their organizations, operative Masons began admitting men from other trades or professions. Because practicing Masons had accepted these men without requiring them to be stoneworkers, these non-practicing members became known as "accepted" Masons. Soon the vast majority of Masons were accepted Masons who came from all walks of life.

Freemasonry, as we know it in America today, began in the 1700s, as wealthy English Masons relocating in the colonies formed lodges through which Masonic influence grew. It flourished throughout America in the early 1800s and by the 1820s was poised to take control of the new nation, with "representatives entrenched at every level of the country's social, economic and political hierarchies."[2] But it suddenly and drastically lost influence and members after the shocking William Morgan affair (see Appendix) only to regain some of its losses as the century progressed. Freemasonry in America seems to have peaked in the 1950s, after which its membership has decreased. Although it is no longer necessary for the Masonic organization to keep trade secrets, it still remains very secretive about select information.

It has secret handshakes, passwords, signs, and tokens by

---

2. From "One Man Exposed the Secrets of the Freemasons. His Disappearance Led to Their Downfall," by Martin Stezano, See: https://www.history.com/news/freemason-secrets-revealed (accessed 9/17/2024).

Looking Back: Historical Perspectives

which Masons identify other Masons and are permitted to visit other lodges. The exact language and actions of its degree rituals are not divulged. Its pagan blood oaths are very carefully hidden from non-Masons, since they are archaic, macabre, and obviously un-Christian. And there are other Masonic secrets never shared outside the Masonic lodge.

For example, I asked a North Carolina Masonic lecturer the identity of Freemasonry's "Lost Word," to which he quickly replied, "Can't tell you that." So, I asked him to confirm some of the details of the first three (Blue Lodge) Masonic degree ceremonies. "Can't tell you that either." I then asked if Masons, when pledging to keep the Craft's secrets, were still required to take blood oaths. His response was the same. Which, of course, strongly implied they *are* still taking blood oaths, or he would have had no reason to be secretive.

Naturally, I wondered, why all this stonewalling? Modern speculative Freemasons run no risk of losing their livelihood if their Craft's secrets become known, as the original operative Masons of Europe did. So, if, as they claim, Freemasons have nothing to hide, if there is nothing dark, strange, anti-Christian, cultish, or even satanic in their core beliefs and rituals, why all the secrecy? Why all the evasion? Why not bring it all out into the light so there may be a robust and profitable objective public debate?

Not one Masonic source I examined gave a legitimate reason for this continued secrecy. This is one of the primary features of Freemasonry true Christians find objectionable. And rightly so. Why keep so many things secret if Freemasonry is merely a wholesome fraternal service organization. Why not allow non-Masons to observe Masonic initiation rituals, if they do not entail anything objectionable?[3] Why not disclose the precise wordings in Masonry's solemn "pledges" or "obligations" (their euphemisms for blood oaths)? Why not open all their practices, rituals, meetings, and other secrets for full public observation? The true church does so.[4]

Freemasonry: Like an Ancient "Mystery Religion"

The element of sworn secrecy found in Freemasonry was also a key element in ancient Greco-Roman mystery religions. These non-standard religions required that their initiates swear to not divulge the secrets of their cults.[5] Of them generally, one source states:

> The word mystery is derived from the Greek verb *myein* ("to close"), referring to the lips and the eyes.

---

3. To their credit, Masons allow the public into their lodges for special events, such as the installation of officers, social galas, or fundraising drives. But no non-Mason is permitted to observe their degree rituals.

4. Initially, Christian churches often met in secret by necessity, not choice, since Christianity was an illegal religion in the Roman empire subject to severe, random persecution from A.D. 64 to 313. Today, most evangelical churches do not permit non-believers to receive Holy Communion or adult baptism (or join their memberships), but they may freely observe these public sacraments.

5. The ancient mystery religions (e.g., Cybele, Mithras, Demeter) were religious cults comprised of nonconformists who worshiped gods not in the official Greek or Roman Pantheon. They met in secret, restricted their meetings to initiates, and swore them to secrecy. All their core beliefs and practices were idolatrous, heretical, and damning.

Mysteries were always secret cults into which a person had to be "initiated" (taken in). The initiate was called *mystēs*, the introducing person *mystagōgos* (leader of the *mystēs*). The leaders of the cults included the *hierophantēs* ("revealer of holy things") and the *dadouchos* ("torchbearer"). The constitutive features of a mystery society were common meals, dances, and ceremonies, especially initiation rites. These common experiences strengthened the bonds of each cult.[6]

Interestingly, this description fits Freemasonry in several ways. Freemasonry keeps its members' mouths and non-members' eyes closed; members dare not divulge its secrets and non-members cannot see its degree rituals. Freemasonry places great emphasis on its introductory rites (Blue Lodge Degrees). Its leaders also have religious names, not "revealer of holy things," but similarly high-sounding religious titles, such as, "worshipful master" (leader of the local lodge). Freemasonry's leaders and members are also considered "torchbearers" in that they alone carry in their hearts the secret, divine, moral "light" of Freemasonry. And Freemasonry's fraternal bonds are strengthened by its many ceremonious procedures and (often) verbose lectures (Lambskin Apron Talk, Funeral Talk, and so forth).

Some Freemason authorities see Freemasons as the modern practitioners of the ancient mystery religions. These present-day "philosophic few" are able to "bear the light" formerly disclosed only to the chosen few who

---

6. See "Mystery Religion," https://www.britannica.com/topic/mystery-religion (accessed 6/24/24).

long ago were favored to receive the esoteric knowledge offered in mystery religions:

> "They [mystery religions] permitted, therefore," says a learned writer on this subject, "the multitude to remain plunged as they were in the depth of a gross and complicated idolatry; but for those *philosophic few* who could *bear the light of truth* without being confounded by the blaze, they removed the mysterious veil, and displayed to them the Deity in the radiant glory of his unity. From the vulgar eye, however, these doctrines were kept inviolably sacred, and wrapped in the veil of impenetrable mystery."
>
> The consequence of all this was that no one was permitted to be invested with the knowledge of these sublime truths, until … he had proved himself worthy and capable of receiving the *full light of wisdom*. For this purpose, therefore, those peculiar religious institutions were organized which the ancients designated as the *Mysteries*, and which, from the resemblance of their organization, their objects, and their doctrines, have by Masonic writers been called the "Spurious Freemasonry of Antiquity."[7]

Thus, the author claims "Masonic writers" consider the practitioners of the ancient mystery religions to be the "Freemasons of Antiquity." Please note, however, there is no historically traceable linkage between ancient mystery religions and Medieval Masonry, much

---

7. From Freemason Information: "The Spurious Freemasonry of Antiquity," by Albert G. Mackey, see: https://freemasoninformation.com/masonic-education/books/the-symbolism-of-freemasonry/v-the-spurious-freemasonry-of-antiquity/ (accessed 6/28/2024).

Looking Back: Historical Perspectives

less modern Masonry. But, as we will see, Freemasonry believes and teaches with deep solemnity many legends which it claims link it to ancient events, persons, and organizations ... without a shred of historical corroboration.

FREEMASONS: POSSESSORS OF SECRET WISDOM

In his celebrated book, *The Builders*, the widely known Masonic authority, Joseph Ford Newton, introduced a dangerous thesis:

> A persistent tradition affirms that throughout the ages, and in every land, behind the system of faith accepted by the masses, an inner and deeper doctrine has been held and taught by those able to grasp it.[8]

Newton (1880-1950) advocates divine truth is not fully disclosed by the Bible, and thus by orthodox Christian doctrine. Therefore, he claims, there has always existed a *parallel revelation* of divine truth (in his words, "Hidden Doctrine" or "Secret Wisdom") reserved only for the enlightened few who are worthy to receive it because they seek it in Freemasonry. This was precisely the heresy of the Gnostics, who troubled the early church by claiming they, and they alone, possessed this secret wisdom.

In Scripture, God carefully distinguishes between *revealed* [scriptural] and *secret* [hidden] knowledge:

---

8. Newton, Joseph Ford, *The Builders*, (Richmond, VA; Macoy Publishing), 1979, 52.

> The *secret* [hidden] things belong to the Lord our God; but those things that are *revealed* [in Scripture] belong unto us and to our children forever, that we may do all the words of this law.
> —DEUTERONOMY 29:29

The Bible does not contain an exhaustive revelation of truth. In consummate wisdom, God sovereignly chose which truths to reveal (the Bible) and which to, for the present, conceal. Humanity's persistent attempt to bypass this divinely set barrier and access secret knowledge, or as Newton puts it, this "inner and deeper doctrine," has been for centuries the infamous business of the occult. Newton states this "Secret Doctrine" once taught by the ancient mystery religions is now taught by "modern Masonry," claiming this secret wisdom is "a method of organized spiritual culture" which remains a *valid* "ministry among men."[9] Thus, he holds the discovery of this secret wisdom God has withheld is now "valid," as is Masonry's "ministry" of it through its manifold symbolic teachings. This is an openly occult position. Newton's sources are revealing.

He glowingly endorsed the works of Arthur Edward Waite,[10] an eccentric, American-born poet and mystic. Waite studied esotericism, was involved with occultist sects (Golden Dawn), co-authored the Rider-Waite Tarot Card deck, wrote books on divination, magic, and Kabbalism, and edited a magazine titled, "The Unknown World." Waite, who became a Mason, was

---

9. Ibid., 57, 60.

10. Ibid., 57-60.

convinced "Scottish Rite [Masonry] represented the 'Secret Tradition' of mystical spiritual illumination"[11] and accessed the "Secret Doctrine" paralleling revealed truth. So, we may accurately conclude Waite was an occultist and Newton his ardent advocate!

All the ancient mystery cults, of which Waite and Newton speak so highly, were non-Judaic and non-Christian. Their teachings were non-canonic, and thus uninspired and heretical. They were the fallible teachings of fallen men who believed in false gods, not infallible truths given by the all-knowing true God. Thus, mystery cultists were idolatrous worshipers of false gods and purveyors of false truth claims utterly antithetical to the pure, divine, true truth claims revealed to biblical authors and meticulously preserved in the Old and New Testaments. Freemasonry's unapologetic identification with them is an embarrassing yet revealing admission that they, too, are at base cultish, and bound in heresy, idolatry, and spiritual darkness.

These elements of sworn secrecy and secret wisdom have carried over into other modern cults. For instance, Mormonism's spiritually deluded founder, Joseph Smith, and four other original Mormon "prophets," all joined and enthusiastically supported the Freemasons. Not long afterwards, numerous traits of Freemasonry's secret rituals and symbols just happened to find their way into Mormonism's secret handshakes, passwords, undergarments, temple architectural features, and its

---

11. Wikipedia, "A. E. Waite," see: https://en.wikipedia.org/wiki/A._E._Waite (accessed 7/4/2024).

temple, or "endowment," ceremonies.[12] By God's revelation to the self-professed "prophet," Joseph Smith, of course! (Incidentally, Mormons hold Smith's extrabiblical books to be as fully inspired as the Bible.[13]) Thus, a subtle yet very traceable link exists between the heresies of Mormonism and Freemasonry.

By contrast, no truly Christian organization maintains secret beliefs, handshakes, or rituals, or makes their members swear to never divulge them. Nor do they claim to hold extrabiblical hidden doctrines containing secret wisdom. Painfully aware of this, Masonic apologists repeatedly assert Freemasonry has no secrets. Newton wrote, "Its [Freemasonry's] one great secret is that it has no secret."[14]

---

12. Armstrong, Jamie, "Latter Day Saints and Masons: 5 Fascinating Connections," January 29, 2018, see: https://www.ldsliving.com/latter-day-saints-and-masons-5-fascinating-connections/s/80329 (accessed 6/25/24).

13. Cults often consider their leaders' messages to be revelatory, divine, and infallible. Joseph Smith's primary works are *The Book of Mormon, The Book of Doctrine and Covenants,* and *The Pearl of Great Price.*

14. Newton, Joseph Ford, *The Builders,* 235.

Chapter Two

LOOKING IN: EXAMINING FREEMASONRY'S WORKING PARTS

Having looked back, it is time to look in—inside Freemasonry's current beliefs and practices, probing to discover more facts that will help us assess it accurately. It is unjust to judge an organization merely by what it was. Fairness requires we also learn what it is. Therefore, we will examine some of Freemasonry's present teachings and activities in this chapter and others in the next. Chapter 2 examines: a typical lodge meeting, some of Freemasonry's many myths, its great pride, and its multiple sacred books.

A Typical Masonic Lodge Meeting

In America, Masonic activity is governed by the Grand Lodge of each state. Local lodges have some freedom to innovate, but not in core beliefs and rituals. So, the following information, though generally accurate, may vary from state to state and, locally, from lodge to lodge.

American Masons usually have a regular, or business, meeting one to four times monthly. Some lodges share a meal beforehand, while others only have refreshments before or after sessions. Masons typically wear business attire and their distinctive white lambskin aprons during these meetings. These regular meetings are closed affairs, restricted exclusively to Masons, but lodges also host special meetings (for charitable projects, fundraisers, galas, or installation of officers) to which they invite their families, and occasionally the public. In these special meetings, no secret Masonic speech, symbols, signs, or degree rituals are on display.

William Regal, a Freemason and founder of Freemasons Community Website, offers this description of a typical, or business, Masonic lodge meeting:

> During our lodge meetings, we engage in a variety of activities that cater to our members' interests, personal growth, and commitment to helping others …
>
> We discuss communications, pay bills, vote on proposed members, and catch up on each other's lives. An essential aspect of these meetings is the performance of ceremonial rituals in which members are initiated or advanced to a higher degree. These rituals serve to foster a deeper understanding of the values and principles underlying our organization, while also building camaraderie among the members.
>
> We dedicate our time to discussing topical issues pertinent to our organization and the world at large. Active engagement in these discussions allows us to gain new perspectives and ultimately contribute to a more harmonious society.
>
> As Freemasons, we value not just the rituals and ceremonies that take place during our meetings, but the opportunity to come together as brothers, share our experiences, and work collectively towards a

brighter future. By engaging in these activities, we honor the heritage of our organization and promote ideals of fellowship, personal growth, and commitment to the betterment of society.

At the beginning of each meeting, we perform an opening ritual to set the tone and establish a sacred space for our work. This ritual typically involves the use of symbols and ceremonial tools and is led by the Worshipful Master, the presiding officer of the lodge. Similarly, at the conclusion of our gathering, we perform a closing ritual to signify the end of the meeting and return our focus to the outside world. These rituals create a frame for our activities and ensure that our actions during the meeting are conducted with respect and solemnity.

One of the essential activities we carry out at our meetings is the conferral of degrees. In Freemasonry, there are three degrees that a member can achieve: Entered Apprentice, Fellowcraft, and Master Mason. When a candidate is ready to advance to a higher degree, a formal ceremonial ritual is performed in order to facilitate their progression. During a degree ceremony, the candidate is guided through a series of lessons and symbolic experiences designed to impart wisdom and moral teachings. These ceremonies help strengthen our understanding of the Craft and foster personal growth. Each degree has a unique ceremony, and upon completion, the candidate is recognized as having attained a new level of understanding and commitment within the brotherhood.

The Worshipful Master is the highest-ranking officer in a Masonic lodge and is responsible for presiding over all meetings, ensuring proper conduct and adherence to Masonic regulations. The Worshipful Master is expected to lead by example, demonstrating dedication and commitment to the principles of Freemasonry. The Senior and Junior Wardens act as second- and third-in-command, respectively, and assist the Worshipful Master in fulfilling his duties. Their primary responsibility is to maintain harmony within the lodge and ensure the welfare of its members.[1]

One of the essential aspects of our meetings is the communication and exchange of ideas among the members. It is through these interactions that we foster brotherly love and better understand each other's perspectives. During the meetings, we engage in both formal and informal conversations.

Formal communication takes place during the opening and closing rituals, as well as during the presentation of lectures and degrees. These structured dialogues ensure that the fundamental tenets of Freemasonry, such as brotherly love, relief, and truth, are effectively communicated among the members. Informal communication, on the other hand, occurs during the refreshment period after each meeting. This time is dedicated to fostering camaraderie and building connections among the members. It allows us to discuss various topics of interest, apart from religion and politics, which are considered off-limits in our gatherings to maintain a harmonious atmosphere.

In addition to verbal communication, Freemasons also use symbolic gestures and signs as part of our rich tradition. These symbols, inspired by the tools

---

[1]. Lodges also elect a Secretary and Treasurer.

of stonemasonry, help us convey our values and teachings in a truly unique way. For instance, the "All-Seeing Eye" or Eye of Providence symbolizes the omnipresence and watchfulness of the Great Architect of the Universe. It is through the combination of verbal and symbolic communication that we successfully engage in meaningful conversations and bond with our fellow members. By embracing our unique communication methods and fostering an environment of trust and respect, we help to strengthen the bonds of brotherhood within Freemasonry.[2]

These business meetings take place in the lodge room of the Masonic temple (lodge). In this typically rectangular room, a few rows of seats on three sides surround a black and white checkered floor (Masonic pavement). The spotlighted Masonic altar is in the center of the room. A Masonic Bible (or other Holy Writ) is open on the altar during lodge meetings. The lodge officers (Worshipful Master, Senior Warden, Junior Warden) are seated on one end of the room, while the Tyler, drawn sword in hand, sits in a small antechamber outside the lodge door to allow only properly credentialed persons to enter. Near the officers, or on either side of the lodge door, are two freestanding pillars, Jachin and Boaz. Named after the pillars that stood outside the door of King Solomon's temple, these two pillars hold diverse symbolic meanings for Masons.[3] Universal Masonic symbols, such as the

---

2. Freemasons Community Website, "What Do Freemasons Do At Meetings (An Insider's Perspective)," by William Regal, see: https://freemasonscommunity.life/what-do-freemasons-do-at-meetings/ (accessed 9/20/2024).

3. In researching the symbolic meanings of Jachin ("He will establish") and Boaz ("In him [the Lord] is strength") (2 Chronicles 3:17), I quickly realized that these two pillars symbolize many things to

square and compass, ubiquitous Masonic "G," all-seeing (or providential) eye, pentagram, crescent moon, and many others, are often present. Finally, two "ashlar" stones, one rough cut and the other smooth, are in a highly visible location, usually near the lodge officers. We will describe their symbolic meaning in Chapter 3.

FREEMASONRY'S MYTHS

Without a doubt, Freemasons are guilty of what Enlightenment critics falsely accused Christians of doing: teaching myths instead of critically verifiable facts. Masons unashamedly teach multiple legends with utmost reverence, as if they were gospel truth.

For instance, in the instructions regarding the "Cryptic Masonry" Degree, the Masonic Heirloom Bible states:

> The term "Crypt" signifies a concealed place, or a subterranean vault ... Within these subterranean hiding places [supposedly under the ruins of the Temple of Solomon] were preserved some of the most sacred and meaningful secrets relating to

---

Masons. To some, they represent "the strong foundations upon which the Masonic tradition is built ... stability and wisdom"; or "strength, stability, and divine support"; or "the balance between opposing forces, such as light and darkness or strength and beauty"; or they "store and protect knowledge"; or they are "a perpetual reminder of the sacred bond between the material and spiritual world"; or they symbolize "the dual virtues of wisdom and fortitude." And I could go on! Suffice it to say, the Jachin and Boaz pillars often mean whatever a Mason wants them to mean! See: https://masonicvibe.com/masonic-pillars/ (accessed 10/15/24). See: https://freemasonrymatters.co.uk/index.php/boaz-and-jachin-from-solomons-temple-to-freemasonry-unraveling-the-symbolism/ (accessed 10/15/24). See: https://www.freemason.com/behind-the-symbol-the-twin-masonic-pillars/ (accessed 10/15/24).

Ancient Craft Masonry.[4]

This myth claims some of the most sacred secrets of "Ancient Craft Masonry" were hidden in the crypts under the ruins of Solomon's temple.[5] It holds these lost secrets of temple construction were later found by men Masons believe were the predecessors of Medieval operative Masonry and modern speculative Masonry. These secrets, which are the basis for many Masonic teachings today, are purported to have belonged to the builder of Solomon's temple, one "Hiram Abiff,"[6] whom modern Masons allege was murdered. For the record, Hiram (or Huram), a Phoenician architect, was a real Bible character (2 Chronicles 2:13).

Also, for the record, all the rest of the intricately designed Hiram Abiff story, which is woven into the

---

4. *The Holy Bible, Heirloom Family Edition*, "The Internal Workings of Freemasonry: Royal Arch Masonry and the York Rite, Cryptic Masonry [Degree]," (Wichita, KS; Heirloom Bible Publishers), 1988, 12.

5. This massive underground man-made cavern, known as the Cave of Zedekiah or Solomon's Quarries (or, to Josephus, the Royal Caverns), was once used to quarry limestone for construction in ancient Jerusalem. It extends from the Damascus Gate some 650 feet (and 30 feet under the street level) to (or near) the ancient temple mount. Accessible today to tourists, it is considered hallowed ground by Freemasons, who first held secret meetings there in 1868 and meet there annually to this day. See: https://www.ancient-origins.net/news-ancient-places-europe/cave-zedekiah-secret-grotto-jerusalem-003492 (accessed 10/14/2024).

6. Hiram's proper name is "Huram-Abi" or "Huram-Abiv" (Martin Luther translated, "Huram-Abif") meaning Master Huram. This title referred to his position as a foreign architect employed to help the Jewish architects construct the great temple God personally designed and revealed to David, who then inscribed its plans by inspiration and passed them on to Solomon (1 Chronicles 28:11-12, 19).

moral lessons conveyed throughout Masonry's various degrees, symbols, and lectures, is false. Pure legend. Uncorroborated history. Humanly contrived nonsense. A tall tale worthy of Joseph Smith, Mormonism's famous spinster of fictional religious history. Without being impolite, it is nevertheless true, that the legend of Hiram Abiff is more fit for Grimm's Fairy Tales than for teaching intelligent, well-educated, grown men character forming life lessons. That is the Bible's unique calling and it discharges that duty peerlessly and perfectly. But there is another deceitful element at play here.

By using Bible characters, events, and texts, including the words of Jesus, as oft-repeated central components of its moral teachings, Freemasonry leads naïve, scripturally untaught Christian Masons to assume they are receiving Christian instruction. Solomon is in the Bible, right? Yes. His temple is in the Bible, right? Yes. Hiram is in the Bible, right? Yes. So, Masonry's Hiram Abif story is biblical and true, right? No! It is unreality posing as reality, babble masquerading as Bible, a fictional tale built upon factual persons and events.

Hollywood does the same thing when it produces a movie "based on" a true story. A story truly happened in real life, but that's not at all the story depicted on the silver screen! The same is true of Hiram. He truly existed in real life and helped construct Solomon's temple. But that's not at all the story depicted in Masonic lore.

Freemasons also see themselves as continuing the tradition of the Knights Templar Medieval order. This order of warrior monks was created in France in the twelfth century (1119) to defend Christians on pilgrimage to the Holy Land who, on the roads leading to Jerusalem, were being robbed and killed by marauders. The Templars also played a key role in the Crusades. They soon established a headquarters and financial center on the recently retaken temple mount in Jerusalem. Non-combatant European Templars began holding funds in trust for noblemen embarking on Holy Land pilgrimages. Naturally, they charged a fee. They also gave these travelers letters of credit for the wealth they deposited. Once in Jerusalem, these pilgrims presented their letters at the Templars' office and received the equivalent in local currency for their use. This arrangement made the pilgrims much less appealing targets to bandits, since they had little money on their persons while traveling. It also constituted an early form of our modern banking (check writing) system.

As the Templars opened offices throughout Europe and the Middle East, they gradually accumulated vast sums of wealth. Coveting this wealth, and desiring to be free of his own large indebtedness to the Templars, King Phillip IV of France allegedly spread damning rumors about the order's secret ceremonies. He also engaged the powerful assistance of Pope Clement V, who, in 1307 issued a papal bull ordering all Templars arrested, their offices closed, and assets seized. In 1312, another papal decree officially dissolved the order. Its last Grand Master, Jacques de Molay, was executed in 1314.

Admiring the Templars' courage, morality, and loyalty, Masons created a special Masonic order honoring them. In 1791, the York Rite Masonic body was formed in England. The Knights Templar Masonic order is a part of the York Rite (though some are separate). Although

Knights Templar Masons officially acknowledge no historical evidence links them to the Medieval Knights Templar order, by persisting in so overtly emulating them in their degrees, instruction, and ceremonies, they create the illusion that they are. Thus, another Masonic legend, though weaker, lives on.

Still another example of Masonic legend is its "Lost Word," which is also supposed to have been lost when Hiram Abiff was murdered:

> There is a Masonic myth that there was a certain word which was lost and afterwards recovered ... It is not material what the word was, nor how lost, nor when recovered: the symbolism refers only to the abstract idea of a loss and a recovery ... It is a symbol of *divine truth*.[7]

In this quote, Albert G. Mackey (MD), another Masonic authority, acknowledges there was no "Lost Word," nor has Freemasonry recovered it. Yet the Craft claims this lost word is either "divine truth," as Mackey holds, or the divine One—the name of God. God has various authentic biblical names, the chief of which is "Yahweh" (or "Lord" in modern translations). But neither the "divine truth" of the entire Bible, nor the biblical name "Yahweh," have ever been lost. These are the facts.

Freemasonry, however, prefers its fiction. It claims the

---

7. Mackey, Albert G., *The Symbolism of Freemasonry*, (New York, NY; Clark and Maynard), 1882, PDF, "Synoptical Index." See: https://archive.org/details/MackeyAGEncylopediaOfFreemasonryVols121914_201705/Mackey%20A%20G%20-%20The%20Symbolism%20Of%20Freemasonry%20-%201882/ (accessed 9/24/2024).

"Lost Word," or name of God, is "Jahbulon."[8] This strange moniker is a combination of the abbreviated names of the deities of three religions:

- YAHWEH, the only true God (and Judeo-Christian deity)

- BAAL, a chief Canaanite deity worshiped by one of Israel's worst ancient enemies (Philistines)

- OSIRIS, the fertility god of an ancient Egyptian mystery religion

Though false, this composite name is very fitting. Since Freemasonry attempts (as we shall see) to blend all religions into the one religion of Freemasonry, it is not surprising they would devise a synthesized name of their supposed deity to head their syncretistic religion.[9]

---

8. Carlson, Ron, Decker, Ed, *Fast Facts on False Teachings*, (Eugene, OR; Harvest House Publishers), 1994, 86.

9. Numerous Masonic sources vigorously reject this claim that "Jahbulon" is the (or a) distinctive name of Freemasonry's god. Among them was Albert Mackey: "In an article on the word 'Bel,' Masonic encyclopedist Albert Mackey tells us 'It [Bel] has, with Jah and On, been introduced into the Royal Arch as a representative of the Tetragrammaton [the Hebrew letters YHWH or JHVH, i.e., Jehovah], which it and the accompanying words have sometimes ignorantly been made to displace. At the session of the General Grand Chapter of the United States, in 1871, this error was corrected; and while the Tetragrammaton was declared to be the true omnific word, the other three were permitted to be retained as merely explanatory.'" So, Mackey says Yahweh (Jehovah) is Freemasonry's official name for its "omnific" (all-creating) deity, yet simultaneously acknowledges the General Grand Chapter intentionally let Jahbulon remain in its Royal Arch instruction. This falls short of a full repudiation. If Jahbulon (or Jah, Bel, and On) is *not* a (or one of the) Masonic moniker(s) for god, why leave it in Masonic degree language? Why not eradicate it from all Masonic texts? This is

As shown above, the name Jah-bul-on fuses the abbreviated names of Yahweh, Baal, and Osiris as follows: Jah, for Yahweh; Bul, for Baal; and On, for Osiris.[10] No born-again, biblically literate Christian would ever accept such a false divine being or name.

To the contrary, all genuine Christians love *truth*, not myths, and will summarily reject all legends presented as valid means of teaching vital moral life lessons.[11] The apostle Peter asserted, "We have *not* followed cunningly devised fables [lit., fiction; myths]" (2 Peter 1:16). And the apostle Paul described those who "turn their ears away from the truth and turn aside to myths" as being *heretics* (2 Timothy 4:4, NIV).

FREEMASONRY'S GREAT PRIDE: ITS "GOOD" MEN, HIGH MORAL CODE, AND EXALTED TITLES

Freemasonry's "Good" Men

Freemasonry accepts only new members whom it deems "good" men and unapologetically excludes those needing to be redeemed or reformed.[12] It requires only one

---

typical Masonic ambiguity—something intentionally designed to be obscure so as to allow plausible deniability. Therefore, I find Mackey's defense unconvincing. For Mackey quote, see: http://web.archive.org/web/20090801085645/http://www.srmason-sj.org/web/SRpublications/deHoyos-chapter3.htm (accessed 10/15/24).

10. Carlson, Ron, Decker, Ed, *Fast Facts on False Teachings*, 86.

11. The exception to this is biblical allegory, which, unlike human mythology (and Masonic legend), is divinely inspired and has a very real historic, present, or prophetic application (Ezekiel 23:1-49; Luke 15:1-10; Rev. 12:1-17).

12. The Grand Lodge of North Carolina, "Freemasonry Revealed: Free-

thing of its good men: they must believe in a god—any god of any religion, or even an unknown, unnamed supreme being.[13]

Masonry's embrace of any god of any religion implies that "good" men are found in *all* religions. This is carnal reasoning, or the viewpoint of unredeemed, not redeemed, men. Two monumental facts render it anti-biblical: Adam's fall and Christ's redemption. It is also an un-Christlike opinion.

Jesus taught there are "none good but one, that is, God" (Matthew 19:17), meaning there are no thoroughly, intrinsically good human beings in God's eyes. However upright we may behave, there is something incorrigibly corrupt deep within us. (Hence, all the trouble in our lives, others', and human history!) Enlarging upon Jesus' teaching, Paul taught that "all" Adam's offsprings are by nature sinners, rebellious toward, disbelieving in, and separated from God. Therefore all "have sinned, and come short of the glory of God" (Romans 3:23). So, the Bible's point of view is that every human being is at

---

masonry and Religion," by Reynold S. Davenport (1980), see: https://www.grandlodge-nc.org/freemasonry-revealed (accessed 6/12/2024).

13. While in Athens, the apostle Paul noticed an altar dedicated "TO THE UNKNOWN GOD" and described this purported deity as "him whom ye ignorantly worship" (Acts 17:23). One New Testament scholar notes, "Athenian tradition declared that during an ancient plague sacrifices to all known deities failed to end the plague. The Cretan Epimenides ... advised the Athenians, and they built altars to unknown gods." Similarly, Masonry allows its members to venerate an "unknown god" as ignorantly as the ancient Athenians did theirs. On quote, see: Keener, Craig S., Walton, John H., *NIV Cultural Backgrounds Study Bible*, (Grand Rapids, MI; Zondervan), 2016, Acts 17:23, note, 1913.

core not good but sinful. Why? Our inherited Adamic sin nature is prone not to goodness but sinfulness; not to trust God but to disbelieve Him; not to submit to but rebel against His will. In this natural, fallen, unregenerated state, all men are at enmity (hostility) not union with God.

For this reason, as Jesus said, no once-born man is "good" and thus acceptable to God. And for this reason, Jesus taught *all* men—whether behaving badly or uprightly—are inwardly so spiritually and morally corrupted with sin that we *all* "must" be "born again," or recreated in our hearts and given a new spirit by repenting of our sins and receiving Christ's nature (John 1:12-13; 3:7). Only then can we, as born-again Christians, begin to learn and live in "goodness" (uprightness, righteousness) as God sees it. Therefore, God could not possibly consider anyone worshiping another god and following another religion, Freemason or not, to be "good." And there is more to this.

Masons regularly hear themselves and other Masons described as "good" men. Soon, consciously or subconsciously, they begin feeling proud of themselves, as if they are a cut above common sinners in need of a Savior. None would dare say this, but it is the unavoidable consequence of hearing this goodness theme repeated again and again with almost mesmeric repetition.[14] Ironically, all this goodness talk is not good! Why? It discourages Masons, especially if they follow a non-Christian god

---

14. Every time a Mason is asked to describe what Freemasonry is or does, his first response is invariably, "We make good men better." This recurring claim, variously worded, appears in virtually every Masonic book, article, video, and website.

and religion, from seeking a spiritual rebirth experience by grace alone through faith alone in Christ alone and His cross alone. If they continue in this state, however clean living and humanly ethical, they will die *lost*—separated from God, denied heaven, bound for hell, and "good" only in their own overinflated self-estimate!

Freemasonry's High Moral Code

Masonic writings boast of the Craft's high moral code. Masons are expected to obey this body of Masonic teaching with complete devotion and faithfulness to their last day on earth. They are promised (as discussed later) that by doing so they will become spiritually and morally mature men and be granted eternal life in the next world. This sounds so good, so admirable, so right! But there is something desperately wrong with it.

Doesn't the *Bible* present the highest moral code in the Ten Commandments, Jesus' teachings, and the New Testament epistles? The apostle Paul certainly thought so:

> *All scripture* is given by inspiration of God, and is profitable [useful] for doctrine, for reproof, for correction, for *instruction in righteousness*, that the man of God may be *perfect* [spiritually and morally fully developed, complete, and mature], *thoroughly furnished* unto all good works.
>
> —2 Timothy 3:16-17

But we must decide for ourselves. Is the Bible a sufficient guide to righteous thought and behavior or not? Let us consider well our answer. If we say "yes," we acknowledge no additional behavior code is necessary to become spiritually and morally mature, and the Masonic code is therefore at best superfluous and at worst competitive. If we say "no," the implications are monstrous: God has failed to give us an adequate code for living in the Bible, and therefore another, of our own design, is needed. Hence, the Masonic code. Or so Masons believe. But it is they, not God, who have failed.

Freemasonry is repeating the profound error of the first century Jewish Pharisees: teaching the commandments of men as if they were the very commandments of God. Rather than confirm the proud Pharisees' moral code—the Oral Law[15]—Jesus pointedly *collided* with it, time and again. Why? The Oral Law was replacing God's Word in the people's minds, leaving God's Word with comparatively little influence over them. And this deception was strengthened greatly by many years of

---

15. In the 2nd Century B.C., the Pharisees understood correctly that disobedience to God's law caused their terrible Babylonian Captivity. They incorrectly assumed, however, they should usurp God's prerogatives by establishing their own humanly contrived rules to supplement His divinely inspired statutes. They "fenced" God's written Law (the Torah) by making their Oral Law (an extensive set of detailed rabbinic applications of the written Law) *more* strict than His. Their rationale was the Jews would break through their "fence" before trespassing God's Law, thus decreasing their offenses against Him. All this sounded good to the Pharisees and their Jewish constituents. After all, they just wanted to help God. In actuality, however, they were hindering God's purposes by acting in unrecognized religious arrogance: they put themselves in God's place and established binding rules He never authored. Thus, while claiming to preserve God's authority, they were usurping and thus defying it! And their hubris only grew. Soon they convinced themselves that their Oral Law was not as but *more* important than God's Law. Masons have done the same by promising salvation to men who keep their code whether or not they receive Jesus; and by promising spiritual and moral maturity to men apart from spiritual rebirth, receiving the Holy Spirit, and obeying the New Testament.

instruction by that most beguiling of teachers, religious tradition! Jesus summed it up, "Why do ye also transgress the commandment of God by your tradition ... teaching for doctrines the [mere] commandments of men" (Matthew 15:3, 9). By venerating its own moral code for hundreds of years, Freemasonry has strengthened the deception it holds over its constituents. Millions of Masons in their hearts consider Masonic code to be as or more authoritative than God's Word.

Freemasonry's Exalted Titles

The titles given Masonic leaders are by any sober estimate overblown. The leader of the local (or Blue) lodge is called, "Worshipful Master." The leader of the regional lodge is a "Grand Master." The leader of a grand (or state) lodge is the "Right Worshipful Grand Master." Scottish Rite Freemasonry leaders are called, "Most Excellent Master" and "Super Excellent Master."[16] All Shriners are also Masons. One serving on a Shriners' council is an "Imperial Sir." Other Shriners' titles are "Illustrious Potentate" and "Imperial Potentate" (head of Shriners International). Some would dismiss these bombastic titles as the silliness of men who, by dressing up in top hats (or Shriners' fezzes), colorfully decorated aprons, white gloves, and ornate collars, and by giving and receiving ridiculous titles, are merely innocently reliving their childhoods. But there is something else present.

These over-the-top appellations exude an *air of grandiosity*

---

16. *The Holy Bible, Masonic Heirloom Edition*, 5.

inspired by the spiritually deadly "pride of life" (1 John 1:16). And, just as with Masons proclaiming themselves "good men" with rhythmic repetition, these vaunted titles are designed to inflate, consciously or subconsciously, the self-esteem of their holders and fellow lodge members. Why is this important? A little pride can't hurt anybody.

Think again! Pride is the worst sin in God's sight, because it was Lucifer's sin in the beginning and it moved God to expel him from His presence in heaven. "These six things doth the Lord hate," wrote wise Solomon, and the first item on God's most-hated list is "a proud [lit., *self-lifted*][17] look" (Proverbs 6:16-17). Down the centuries, God, who cannot change (Malachi 3:6; Hebrews 13:8), has never changed His disposition toward the sin of pride: no self-promoting person will ever stand in His presence. Realizing this, no truly born-again, God-fearing, Spirit-taught, trial-humbled Christian would dare allow his fellows to address him with such pompous titles, nor would he address others with them.

Masons may respond by accusing Christians of using self-lifting titles when they refer to their ministers as "Reverend" or "Right Reverend." (In Catholicism, "Your Eminence," or when addressing the Pope, "Holy Father" or "Your Holiness.") And they have a point. Do we really need these traditional appellations? Do they help or harm us? Why not simply use the biblical names of "pastor," "bishop," or "elder" for our ministers? But try

---

17. Strong, J., *A Concise Dictionary of the Words in the Greek Testament and The Hebrew Bible*, (Bellingham, WA; Logos Bible Software), 2009, s. v. "rûwm."

as I may, I simply cannot imagine any assembly of re-generated, spiritually minded, Bible-taught, Christian disciples addressing their pastor as "Worshipful Master" or their superintendent as "Imperial Potentate."

FREEMASONRY'S MULTIPLE SACRED BOOKS

American Freemasons require a Bible be opened on the Masonic altar every time local lodges are in session. Each state, however, determines precisely which translation or edition of the Bible is to be used in its jurisdiction. But this is not the case outside the United States. For instance, in Great Britain and Europe, where biblical Christianity is in decline and secularism is ubiquitous, some lodges no longer require a Bible be present.

In other nations where Christianity is not the primary religion, Masons are free to place the holy writings of different religions on their altars. In India, for instance, one of the Hindu Vedas may be used; in Turkey or Pakistan, the Islamic Koran; in Japan, the Shinto Kojiki; in Malaysia, the Buddhist Pali canon; and so forth. They do not have to use these religious texts, but the point is, they may. This very intentional *mixture* of religious texts sends a quiet but clear message: all gods and religions are essentially the same and lead one to the same god![18]

---

18. In the prestigious Scottish Rite House of the Temple in Washington, D.C., four holy books sit atop the altar in its lodge room: The Holy Bible, the Jewish Tanakh, the Muslim Quran, and the Hindu Bhagavad Gita. This display is an overt, powerful symbol of the heresy "all gods and religions lead to the same god." This will undoubtedly be taught in one or another form by the harlot church and one-world religious system that will rise in the Tribulation (Revelation 17) and ultimately worship the Antichrist.

Born-again Christians believe the Bible alone is the truly inspired Word of God and all other Holy Writs are false texts authored by false prophets praising false gods and promoting false ways of salvation. By mixing inspired and non-inspired writings, Freemasonry is leading Masons into a quagmire of lethal spiritual and theological confusion. The Apocrypha published in Roman Catholic and Orthodox Bibles create similar confusion. Readers wonder if, or which, Apocryphal texts hold binding authority; or worse, they believe all are binding.

We find a similar mixing of infallible and fallible texts in pseudo- or quasi-Christian cults. As footnoted earlier, Mormons hold three works authored by their founder, Joseph Smith, to be as equally inspired as the Bible.[19] The Seventh Day Adventists also hold the error-riddled books of their founder, Ellen G. White, equal to the Bible.[20] The same mingling of genuinely and disingenuously inspired texts on Masonic altars around the world confuses undiscerning Masons. They are inclined to accept holy and heretical teachings as having equal authority, the Holy Writs of other religions as being no less true than the Judeo-Christian Bible. And why? The good judgment of the good men in their good lodge could never misidentify God's Good Book(s)!

---

19. They are *The Book of Mormon, The Book of Doctrine and Covenants,* and *The Pearl of Great Price.*

20. They are *The Great Controversy, Steps to Christ,* and *The Desire of Ages.*

Chapter Three

LOOKING DEEPER: EXAMINING FREEMASONRY'S CORE HERESIES

Having looked in, we will now look deeper—into the very heart of Freemasonry's teachings and practices. We need to more fully and accurately know what they are, so we may make a well-informed, thoroughly considered decision as to whether we should seek or flee the lodge. Continuing our probe begun in Chapter 2, this chapter takes a deeper look at the worst Masonic errors. Specifically, we will explore its false light claims, most deadly heresy, identity as a religion, vision of world transformation, remnants of racism, blood oaths, and link to Shriners—and Islam.

FREEMASONRY'S FALSE LIGHT CLAIMS

The first ritual a Masonic initiate experiences is, well, enlightening! Blindfolded, his left pant leg rolled up above the knee, his shirt opened to expose his left breast, his right shoe replaced with a slipper, a sword pressed to his chest, and a noose placed around his neck (how cultish!), the initiate is led to the door of the lodge by a Masonic officer. Then he is led into the lodge's darkened main chamber where a light shines down on an altar. Bowing down at the altar before the "Worshipful

Master," he says, in so many words, "I am lost in darkness and I am seeking the light of Freemasonry."[1]

The Masonic Bible states, "Of his own free will and accord he petitions the Lodge, and seeks admission that he may *begin* his search for Light, the *light of divine Truth*."[2] This authoritative source shows definitively that Masons believe the light they hold is "divine Truth" and the initiate is only *beginning* his search for it. This implies that, prior to this initiation rite, he has *not* found the light of divine truth anywhere outside Freemasonry—including Christianity! No true Christian could say this, as it would be a denial of his having *already* found the Light of the world in Christ, His Word, and His church. It would further be a confirmation that the light of divine truth is *only* found within the Masonic lodge and its teachings, and that within the lodge any Mason of any religion worldwide may access true divine truth *without* being born again by grace through faith in Christ's redemption. This is a blasphemous denial of Christ's cross, rendering His incarnation unnecessary, His death futile, the Gospel a farce, Christians deceived, and the church a purveyor of falsehood.

The Freemason lecturer I interviewed denied Masonic "light" is divine revelation, insisting it is only a metaphor for the knowledge, wisdom, and life guidance of Masonic teaching that enables good Masons to become better men, brothers, husbands, and fathers. Obviously,

---

[1]. Carlson, Ron, Decker, Ed, *Fast Facts on False Teachings*, 74-75.

[2]. *The Holy Bible. Heirloom Family Edition,* 10.

he was being dishonest, because he has surely read the primary Masonic resources I accessed. But he was being partially accurate. Masons emphasize that their instruction matures men spiritually and morally. But even this claim is heretical. It claims the inspired teachings of Jesus and His apostles in the New Testament are not sufficient to make good Christians better men or, in theological terms, to sanctify them. And it implies Freemasonry discharges that sacred instruction better than the church.

The question we should ask is not how Masonic sources or lecturers define Masonic "light," but how Jesus, the Light of the world, and the holy Scriptures, define it, since they alone give us God's perspective. Jesus repeatedly used "light" to refer to *divine* illumination.

Consider these seven questions and their definitive biblical answers describing divine light:

Question #1

Is it not true that God Himself—Yahweh, the true God, and Father of Jesus Christ, and not the generic, unbiblical Masonic deity—is the ultimate Source and Giver of divine Light?

> This then is the message which we have heard of him [God], and declare unto you, that *God is light*, and in Him is no darkness at all.
>
> —1 John 1:5

Question #2

Is it not true that Jesus, not Masonic teaching, embodies this divine Light?

I am *the light of the world*. He who follows me shall not walk in darkness, but have the [only] *light of life*.
—John 8:12, NKJV

Question #3

Is it not true that biblical, not Masonic, teaching defines "light" (divine illumination) for us?

The entrance of *your words* give *light*; it gives understanding [life insight] to the simple.
—Psalm 119:130, NKJV

Your words are a doorway that lets in light, giving understanding to the thoughtless.
—Psalm 119:130, CJB

Question #4

Is it not true that Christians are called to walk in the light of Jesus' righteousness, not that of the Masonic code?

If we walk in *the light*, as *he is in the light*, we have fellowship one with another.
—1 John 1:7

Question #5

Is it not true that Christ, not Masonry, is the sole Repository of the light of divine wisdom and knowledge?

Christ, in whom are hid *all* the [*light*] treasures of wisdom and knowledge.
—Colossians 2:2-3

Question #6

Is it not true that all these facets of divine light—God the Father, Christ, Scripture, righteousness, wisdom, knowledge of God—are found *only* in the body of born-again believers worldwide, in whom Christ lives, not in the Masonic fraternity, or the world's other religions?

> You [born-again Christians] are the *light* of the world ... let *your light* so shine before men, that they may see your good works, and glorify your Father in heaven.
>
> —Matthew 5:14-16

Question #7

Is it not true that we discover divine light, not when we are initiated into Freemasonry, but when we receive Christ and are baptized into His church?

> In the past you were full of darkness, but now you are *full of light in the Lord.* Live as children who *have* [already found true] *light.*
>
> —Ephesians 5:8, NCV

These multiple, definitive biblical texts lead us to only one conclusion:

Freemasonry bears false light from another, non-divine source. And that source can only be Satan, whose original name was Lucifer, or "light bearer." The apostle Paul warned us of his deceptive activities, most specifically that Satan, and the messengers through whom he speaks to this sin-darkened world, always pose as "angel[s] of light" offering divine truth and righteousness:

> Satan disguises himself as an angel of light. Therefore, it is not surprising if his servants also disguise themselves as servants of righteousness.
> —2 CORINTHIANS 11:14-15, NAS

So, Freemasonry professes to offer light when in reality it dispenses spiritual darkness. It claims its source is divine when it is actually diabolical. It claims to lead its initiates into the light when in fact it leads them further into darkness.

Ironically, some leading Masonic authorities acknowledge many lower-level Master Masons, who comprise the Craft's vast majority, are still in the dark as to Freemasonry's core, heretical, philosophical and religious beliefs. The information is widely available but, strangely, they have never researched it. "It is a lamentable fact that the mass of our membership are ignorant of everything connected with Freemasonry," wrote Roland Blackmore.[3] George H. Steinmetz admitted, "The average Mason is lamentably ignorant of the real meaning of the Masonic symbols, and knows as little of its esoteric teachings."[4]

The heavyweight, prolific Masonic Scholar, Albert Pike, went farther, claiming he and other Masonic writers have *intentionally* kept their Blue Lodge brethren in the dark:

---

3. Carlson, Ron, Decker, Ed, *Fast Facts on False Teachings*, 77.

4. Ibid.

Looking Deeper: Examining Freemasonry's Core Heresies

> The Blue [first three] Degrees are but the outer court or portico of the temple. Part of the symbols are displayed there to the Initiate, but he is *intentionally* misled by false interpretations. It is *not intended* that he shall imagine that he understands them.[5]

This quote exposes Pike's deep disdain for the brotherhood he swore to lovingly defend and honor with utmost loyalty. And he has more to say:

> Their [Blue Lodge Degrees] true explication is reserved for the Adepts, the Princes of Masonry ... It is well enough for the mass of those called Masons to imagine that all is contained in the Blue Degrees ... [But] Masonry, like all the religions, all the mysteries [ancient Mystery religions], *conceals* its secrets from all except the adepts and sages, or the elect, and uses false explanations and misinterpretations of its symbols to mislead those who deserve only to be misled ... Truth is not for those who are unworthy or unable to receive it, or would pervert it.[6]

Without the slightest reservation, Pike calmly acknowledges that, in designing the text of the Blue Lodge (or first three) Degrees, esoterically astute Masonic authors have purposely used obscure language that makes their symbolism, while impressive, uninterpretable to people of average intellectual perception. Only the most skilled, or wisest, the "adepts and sages," will discern what they truly mean. Pike's arrogance here is breathtaking. It is esotericism in its haughtiest form—openly

---

5. Ibid, 79.

6. Ibid, 79-80.

mocking ordinary people and declaring only the most elite, highly degreed Masons worthy to comprehend the true "light" the Craft proffers the ignorant masses. May every Mason reading this stop and ponder the ugly spirit at the core of the Craft. Why would you submit your soul to Masonic philosophers, such as Pike, who have only contempt for you?

May this exposé enlighten many Masons whose respected authorities have disrespected them by intentionally keeping them in the dark about the true meaning of Freemasonry's degree rituals—and prevent many others from plunging into its dark deceptions.

FREEMASONRY'S MOST DEADLY HERESY

The most catastrophic false doctrines are those that lead people to perdition in the guise of leading them to paradise. Freemasonry's most egregious heresy is its many antibiblical promises of eternal salvation. Powerless to save, it leads Masons into powerful deception. If they trust in Masonic teaching, it smilingly leads them to not eternal life with God but eternal separation from Him.

Throughout history, a universal, common hallmark of false soteriology[7] has been the unscriptural insistence that salvation is obtained by works, or by grace plus works, but not by grace alone. Virtually every false religion and false Christianity (Catholicism, Mormonism, Adventism) teach one or the other view.

---

7. Soteriology is simply *salvation doctrine*. It explores the ways various religions describe why we need salvation (redemption), how it is provided, and how we receive it.

Masonic soteriology is woven into many of its degrees and lectures. All share a common thread alleging salvation by works, whereas the New Testament teaches only one way of salvation: by grace alone through faith alone in Christ alone and His work alone on the cross alone.

The Lord Jesus asserted this unequivocally:

> I am the way, the truth, and the life. No one comes to the Father except through me.
> —John 14:6, NKJV

The apostle Paul clarified and expanded Jesus' assertion:

> For by grace you have been saved through faith, and that not of yourselves; it is the [free] gift of God, not of works, lest anyone should boast.
> —Ephesians 2:8-9, NKJV

> For you have been delivered by grace through trusting, and even this is not your accomplishment but God's gift. You were not delivered by your own actions; therefore no one should boast.
> —Ephesians 2:8-9, CJB

With this fresh in your mind, we will now examine a few key samples of Masonry's false salvation doctrine found in the Master Mason Degree, Mark Master Degree, Lambskin Apron Lecture, and Funeral Talk.

The Master Mason Degree

Utterly ignoring the fundamental New Testament salvation texts we have just reviewed, and many others, the Master Mason Degree teaches the following:

> The symbolism of the Master Degree ... reaches a climax in *the assurance of a future life*.[8]
>
> Foremost of all the truths taught and emphasized in this Degree is the immortality of the soul of man and the certainty of the resurrection of his body to *eternal life*. The whole scope of the Ritual and the ultimate of the symbols of the Master Mason Degree place supreme emphasis upon the truth that when man's life has spent itself on the earth ... his soul returns to God who gave it and his body which returns to dust shall be *raised, incorruptible and glorified* and *qualified for* entrance into *the Grand Lodge* of the *Celestial City of God* ... [which brings] *ultimate triumph* to every *true, tested, tried, and faithful Master Mason*.[9]

This heresy claims not born-again Christians but *faithful Master Masons* (of all religions) have "the assurance of a future life" and, once resurrected, will enter "eternal life." It also claims "every true, tested, tried, and faithful Mason" will be "qualified" to enter the "Grand Lodge of the Celestial City of God," an intended reference to New Jerusalem (Revelation 21-22). This is the Mason's "ultimate triumph."

Yet the Bible offers no "assurance of a future life" to anyone who does not receive Christ's redemption by grace through faith, nor does the Book of Revelation describe any "Grand Lodge" awaiting faithful Masons

---

8. *The Holy Bible, Heirloom Family Edition,* "The Internal Workings of Freemasonry: Blue Lodge Masonry, The Master Mason Degree," 11.

9. Ibid.

in heaven. Here Masons' mythology and pride are on full display: they imagine a salvation and Grand Lodge that do not exist. They flatter themselves by imagining faithfulness to their Masonic teaching will qualify them to live in God's celestial city ... eternally!

The Mark Master Degree

The Mark Master Degree teaches the following:

> Having been taught the duty of *discharging all the duties of life*, we are now instructed in the importance of *performing them with systematic regularity*. The goal of every true Mark Master is so to *live and work* that he may receive at the conclusion of his services that welcome plaudit, "Well done, thou good and faithful servant; thou hast been faithful over a few things, I will make thee ruler over many things: Enter thou into the joy of thy Lord.[10]

This heresy takes a precious promise of born-again (saved) Christians being rewarded for their post-conversion good works completely out of context (Matthew 25:21, 23). It uses it instead to teach that all Masons who discharge their duties regularly will be *saved* because of their good works. If the Mark Master Mason performs "all the duties of life" with "systematic regularity," then, because he so "live[s] and work[s]," Christ will joyfully receive him into His eternal kingdom: "Well done, thou good and faithful servant ... Enter thou into the joy of thy Lord['s kingdom]." This sounds

---

10. Ibid., "The Internal Workings of Freemasonry: Royal Arch Masonry and the York Rite, Mark Master Degree," 12.

very appealing to idealistic human pride: you can work your way to heaven. Earn salvation. Deserve it. Boast in it!

But there is no mention of the most basic facts of true salvation: our fallenness (total depravity, or inability to save ourselves), conviction of sins, confession of sins, God's redeeming grace, forgiveness of sins through Christ's blood, or the new birth (John 3:3-8). Ignoring these monumental biblical facts, the Mason is promised an honorable entrance into Christ's kingdom for "systematic regularity" in performing his Masonic "duties of life."

Also, this use of *biblical terminology* ("Well done, thou good and faithful servant") without *biblical soteriology* is designed to deceive the biblically uninformed, spiritually undiscerning Christian into thinking his Masonic instruction is Christian instruction. He repeatedly hears Bible verses, persons, incidents, and symbols openly read, not realizing they are being twisted to convey a false message. Thus, he trusts the Masonic "gospel," though it is unbiblical and fatally misleading.

The Lambskin Apron Lecture

The Lambskin Apron Lecture completely misinterprets the Great White Throne Judgment. It tells every new Mason, upon receiving his white, lambskin apron in his local lodge:

> Let its pure and spotless surface be to you an ever-present reminder of purity of life, of rectitude of conduct ... for *higher thoughts,* for *nobler deeds,* for *greater achievements;* and when at last your weary

feet shall have reached the end of their toilsome journey, and from your nerveless grasp forever drop the working tools of a busy life, may the *record of your life and conduct* be as pure and spotless as this fair emblem which I place within your hands tonight; and when your trembling soul shall stand naked and alone before the great white throne, there to receive judgment for the deeds done while here in the body, may it be your portion to hear from Him who sitteth as the Judge Supreme these welcome words: "Well done, thou good and faithful servant, enter thou into the joy of thy Lord."[11]

Again, good works, specifically, "the record of your life and conduct," are said to have not rewarding merit for the saved but saving merit for the lost. "Higher thoughts," "nobler deeds," and "greater achievements" are presented as the means of entering the next life with joy. The Great White Throne Judgment alluded to (Revelation 20:11-15), however, will not decide anyone's salvation or damnation. The righteous—Christians saved by grace through faith—will have already been translated or resurrected over a thousand years earlier in the rapture of the church (1 Corinthians 15:49-53; 1 Thessalonians 4:15-18), after which they will immediately stand before Christ's Judgment Seat (bema). There He will assess their life works as *redeemed Christians* to determine how many eternal rewards they will receive for good works, or forfeit for unworthy works (Romans 14:10; 2 Corinthians 5:10; 2 John 8). The 7-year Tribulation period and 1,000-year Millennium will follow.

---

11. Carlson, Ron, Decker, Ed, *Fast Facts on False Teachings*, 85.

It is *after* the Millennium (Revelation 20:1-10) that the Great White Throne Judgment occurs (20:11-15). In that Judgment, *not one* righteous individual will be resurrected and examined, only the lost. And their works will be assessed, not to determine if they enter God's eternal kingdom, but to determine their degree of punishment in the lake of fire. Therefore, ironically, and tragically, the Lambskin Apron Lecture is unintentionally acknowledging that if Masons put their faith in, not Christ's cross but Masonic doctrine, they will stand before the Great White Throne, not saved but lost. Eternally! And there is more.

The lambskin is yet another subtle biblical link designed to deceive. It is said to represent "purity" of life and a "spotless" record of righteous conduct. Yet no man can achieve this spotless perfection. The Bible declares sinlessly perfect conduct is impossible for fallen man, for "all have sinned and come short of the glory of God" (Romans 3:23). Also, after Adam and Eve sinned, God "clothed them" with "coats of skins" (Genesis 3:21), which symbolized the covering of Christ's righteousness we receive in Christian salvation that enables us to live in God's presence. To provide these skins, God killed an animal. Its blood represents Christ's blood later spilled on the cross as the penalty for the sin of Adam and his race. While the Bible does not identify this animal, it was surely a spotless lamb prefiguring Jesus, the sinless "Lamb of God who takes away the sin of the world" (John 1:29, NKJV). No other sacrifice or obedience can atone for our sins, cleanse the defilement of our sins, free us from the power of sin, or cover us in righteousness.

Again, this biblical link to a "lambskin" causes biblically untaught, spiritually naïve Christians to imagine they are honoring Christ, the spotless Lamb of God, and clothing themselves in His righteousness whenever they wear their lambskin apron. But they are trusting just the opposite, their own righteousness: their "higher thoughts," "nobler deeds," and "greater achievements" presumably to be inscribed in the "record of their life and conduct."

The Funeral Talk

The Masonic Funeral Talk, publicly recited at every Mason's funeral, contains at least four clearly unbiblical Masonic beliefs:

#1 – The departed Mason has entered heaven's "Celestial Lodge."

> The body of our Brother will be committed to the kindly embrace of Mother Earth; in a profound sleep that shall not be disturbed; but his spirit has winged its flight to *that blissful Lodge* which will remain open during the endless ages of eternity … *the Celestial Lodge …*

Without any reference to the departed Mason having received salvation through Christ during his lifetime, this oration assures mourners that his soul has now gone to "the Celestial Lodge" which will "remain open during the endless ages of eternity." This gives false assurance of eternal salvation to the family and friends of deceased Masons who, while perhaps doing good deeds and being religious, never repented of their sins and received Jesus during their lifetime. Also, as previously stated, the Bible describes no Celestial Lodge. This is a Masonic myth, emanating solely from Masonic hubris. So proud are Masons of their lodges that they presumptuously project their earthly institutions right into the very heart of God's heavenly kingdom—without one verse of biblical authority.

#2 – *The departed Mason will "flourish" in God's eternal kingdom.*

> This evergreen [laid on the casket] ... By it we are admonished that we too, like our Brother, shall soon be clothed in the habiliments of death; yet, through the loving kindness of the Supreme Grand Master, *we may confidently hope* that our souls hereafter *flourish in eternal spring* ...

The evergreen branch laid ceremoniously on the departed Mason's casket symbolizes Masons' "confident hope" that their deceased brother will rise and "flourish in eternal spring." But, again, while God's mercies are referred to, Christ's redemption is ignored. Again, this gives false assurance that deceased Masons who never received Christ will "flourish" in God's eternal kingdom. It is good to give mourners uplifting hope in the hour of their grief whenever we may do so. But such hope must be grounded in solid biblical truth, not mere humanistic wishfulness. In eternity, every false salvation hope will be exposed, but it will be too late. We need to see through them now, while there is still time to give all people, the mournful and the merry, the one, true hope of salvation: Christ!

#3 – *The departed Mason's "passions" were subdued by Masonic teaching during his lifetime.*

> The physical being, wherein dwelt the spirit [of the deceased] while upon this earth; that physical being through which, by the *teachings of Masonry* the *passions had been subdued* ...

The Funeral Talk boasts that by "the teachings of Masonry" the bodily "passions" of the departed Mason were "subdued" while he was in this world. This, too, contradicts God's Word. The New Testament tells us "the flesh," or fallen human nature and its passions expressed through the body, may only be "mortified" (deadened, deprived of power) as born-again Christians steadily trust Christ and obey His Word in submission to the Holy Spirit and the guidance of consecrated, spiritually minded ministers (Romans 8:13; Ephesians 4:11-15; 1 Thessalonians 5:12-24). This highlights Freemasonry's great pride in its doctrine. It suggests any Mason of any religion (or no religion) may subdue his carnal nature merely by obeying Masonic teaching—without Christ's salvation, Word, Spirit, and ministers. Thus, it attempts to replace New Testament instruction, specifically on breaking sin's power in the believer's life, with Masonic instruction.

#4 – *Masons do not need Jesus to get to heaven.*

> It has pleased the *Grand Master of the Universe* to summon him into His Eternal presence ... the *Supreme Grand Master* ... the *All-Seeing Eye* ... the *Supreme Architect*.[12]

---

12. There is no central, authoritative text used across America for Masonic Funerals. The grand lodge of each state decides the specific lectures, prayers, and rituals used by its members. They are, however, very similar in substance and, in many cases, order and wording. For this

The mighty, saving name of *Jesus*, the name above all names, is not mentioned in the Funeral Talk. Not once! Peter and John declared "there is no other name under heaven given among men, whereby we must be saved" (Acts 4:12). It is incredible to think that a truly saved man's eulogy would exclude the name of Jesus. To the contrary, most Christians would want Jesus' name openly proclaimed and highly exalted at their funeral. Why? So that any unconverted soul present may hear and receive the true gospel while the Christian's funeral brings them face to face with the natural man's greatest fear and foe, death! But the "gospel" presented at a Masonic funeral refers to God only in non-biblical, generic, Masonic terminology as: the "Grand Master of the Universe," "Supreme Grand Master," "All-Seeing Eye," "Supreme Architect," or the "Great Architect of the universe." Here Masons' excessive self-esteem is again prominently displayed. They presumptuously address God by monikers they have invented, not those He has dictated.[13] This omission

---

study, I quote from the "Masonic Funeral / Wake Service" approved by the Grand Lodge of Connecticut, revised 2002. See: Microsoft Word – funeral_lecture_rev_01.doc, 4-8. The PDF of this lecture, accessed by the URL I have listed, derives from the website "mason33.org" (accessed 9/23/2024).

13. In defense of this charge, some Masonic writers note that, in his *Institutes of the Christian Religion,* John Calvin repeated referred to God as the "Great Architect of the Universe." This is true. But Calvin was speaking *metaphorically*, not literally; he was describing God's actions, not His person. In no reference did Calvin, or any other orthodox Christian theologian, use "Great Architect of the Universe" as a genuine moniker, or proper name, of the God of Israel and the church. The Bible identifies that name clearly and consistently as Yahweh or Elohim (with variations, Yahweh Sabaoth, El-Shaddai, and so forth), or the Godhead personified, Jesus Christ.

of Jesus' name is intentional, since lifting Jesus up may offend non-Christian Masons and mourners. So, stifling the Holy Spirit, Masons offend Jesus by excluding His name from their funeral talks. This silence speaks volumes: *Masons do not need Jesus to get to heaven!*

In conclusion, Masonic salvation doctrine as presented in these degrees and talks urges Masons to trust their good works and faithfulness to Masonic duties to gain them eternal life in the kingdom of God. Like the Book of Mormon written by Joseph Smith, also a Mason, the Masonic gospel is a false gospel. And because it leads men whom God loves to hell instead of heaven, God's anathema is upon it.[14] The apostle Paul's inspired dictum on this subject is definitive and unforgettable:

> Though we, or an angel from heaven, preach any other gospel unto you than that which we have preached unto you [salvation by grace through faith in Christ's redeeming work], let him be accursed."
> —GALATIANS 1:8

So vital, so urgent, was this issue of right vs. wrong salvation doctrine that the great apostle, prompted by the Holy Spirit, restated his grave dictum:

> As we have said before, so say I now again, If any man preach any other gospel unto you than that which ye have received, let him be accursed.
> —GALATIANS 1:9

---

14. Field, Eddy D. II, Field, Eddy D. III, "Freemasonry and The Christian," 153, see: https://tms.edu/wp-content/uploads/2021/09/tmsj5g.pdf (accessed 8/13/2024).

Therefore, all who believe Freemasonry's false gospel bring themselves under not the blessing but the curse of God, not His favor but His wrath, not angelic protection but demonic influence. Rather than finding salvation, they forfeit it.

FREEMASONRY: BY EVERY DEFINITION A RELIGION

While Freemasons freely acknowledge their Craft's religiousness, they repeatedly and emphatically deny it is a religion. Nevertheless, it bears all the earmarks of one. Obviously, Freemason advocates hope we will listen to their repeated denials rather than look at the obvious facts.

The Cambridge Dictionary Online defines "religion" as: *the belief in or worship of a god or gods, or any such system of belief and worship.*[15] With this in mind, let us consider twelve compelling facts about Freemasonry. The lodge:

1. IDENTIFIES A SACRED RELIGIOUS TEXT
2. HAS AN ALTAR IN ITS MEETING ROOM
3. REQUIRES ITS MEMBERS BELIEVE IN A (ANY) GOD
4. OFFERS A NAME FOR (ITS) GOD
5. TEACHES A WAY TO ETERNAL LIFE
6. OFFERS PURPORTEDLY DIVINE LIGHT
7. MEETS IN A TEMPLE
8. CALLS ITS LODGE LEADERS "WORSHIPFUL MASTER"

---

15. The Cambridge Dictionary Online, "religion," see https://dictionary.cambridge.org/ dictionary/english/religion (accessed 8/13/2024).

9. AIMS TO MATURE MEN SPIRITUALLY AND MORALLY

10. ASPIRES TO REFORM THE WORLD

11. USES BIBLE VERSES, SYMBOLS, AND ALLUSIONS TO INSTRUCT

12. MIMICS, AND THUS RIVALS, THE CHURCH'S WORK

This list, and the descriptions below, offer sufficient evidence that Freemasonry possesses "the belief in or worship of a god or gods" and a distinct "system of belief and worship." Therefore, if its spokesmen say a million times it is *not* a religion, the fact remains that it *is*.[16] To deny this is to come to one of two illogical conclusions: (1) the Cambridge Dictionary has defined "religion" incorrectly, or (2) we cannot be sure any other religion is a religion either!

So, let us review these twelve facts. Freemasonry:

1. IDENTIFIES A SACRED RELIGIOUS TEXT. In the most conspicuous location in the lodge, placed reverently on an altar, and always open when the lodge is in session, is a Bible. Or, if the lodge prefers, the Holy Writ of another non-Christian faith. (Or, in rare cases, more than one sacred text.) Everything in this scene speaks of religion and deities. The Bible is the sacred text of the world's largest religion, Christianity, and its deity, Yahweh. Any other Holy Writ presented in its stead is the sacred text of another religion and purported god or gods. Books are written to be read by those desiring to know their content. The very presence of the Bible, or

---

16. Pardon my use of a cliché but, if it swims like a duck, walks like a duck, flies like a duck, and quacks like a duck, it's a duck.

other Holy Writ, implies lodge members desire to know their contents—which invariably disclose the religious instruction of a particular god for its devotees. And, by definition, a god is the primary component of a religion. Non-religious organizations do not center their activities around gods or their Holy Writs.

2. HAS AN ALTAR IN ITS MEETING ROOM. Every lodge has an altar situated prominently in its meeting chamber. Historically, altars have been sacrosanct centerpieces of temples (sanctuaries; shrines) reserved for various religious offerings to gods: prostrations (surrender), prayers, devotion (vows), sacrifices (gifts), or worship. Altars are not found in non-religious settings. The Masonic altar is at the center of its degree rituals. Initiates bow there with deep, reverential respect before the open Bible, as before the presence or view of a god. They "pray" there, petitioning the Worshipful Master and lodge. For example, First Degree initiates ask permission to pass from darkness into the divine "light" of Masonry. Masons also make vows of faithfulness and secrecy at the altar sealed with the most solemn and binding oaths. Thus, in a spirit of worship, they prostrate themselves figuratively, surrendering their wills and offering (gifting) their lives with utmost devotion to their Masonic brothers and duties as to a god, vowing to offer the ultimate sacrificial worship—the shedding of their own blood—if they break their oaths. So, all the basic elements associated with a religion's altar are present in the lodge: surrender, prayer, devotion, vows, sacrifices, and worship.

3. REQUIRES ITS MEMBERS BELIEVE IN A (ANY) GOD. Every Mason must believe in a supreme being. This

may be one whose name is familiar, such as, Yahweh (Jehovah), Allah, a Hindu god, or a less familiar deity. They may even believe in a god whose identity they do not know, such as the "unknown god" to whom the Athenians prayed (Acts 17:23). So, in their theologically all-inclusive philosophy, Masons believe *any* god is as valid as *any other* god, which is another way of saying all purported gods are really the same god. This makes a mockery of Jesus, who boldly claimed He had exclusive access to the only true God: "I am the way, the truth, and the life: no man cometh unto the Father [and true God], but by me" (John 14:6). The apostle Peter also declared Jesus is the *only* way to be saved by the *only* supreme Being: "By the name of Jesus Christ ... for there is no other name under heaven given among men, whereby we must be saved" (Acts 4:10, 12). If the Masonic view is true, Jesus' and Peter's views are false. If all gods are valid, their views are invalid. These are evidently irreconcilable contradictions.

4. Offers a name for (its) god. Freemasonry's most distinctive fraternal emblem found on its buildings, books, and even shirts, is a builder's square and compass with a large "G" in the middle. Most Masons understand this "G" represents God or, more specifically, the generic Masonic god, whom they typically refer to as the "Great Architect of the Universe." But the secretive, more closely guarded Masonic name for the supreme deity is "Jahbulon," as stated earlier. (For the record, the secondary meaning of the Masonic "G" is geometry, a key science in the lives of the original operative Masons, who were stoneworkers.) Only a religion would so openly, centrally, and frequently use an

emblem distinctly representing a deity.

5. TEACHES A WAY TO ETERNAL LIFE. Freemasonry's degree rituals and lectures, as I have described, clearly teach salvation by good works, specifically by faithfully living according to the Masonic code. This, they claim, prepares good Masons—not born-again Christians but once-born Masons—to face final judgment and enter eternal life blissfully. A religion has no greater duty than ushering its adherents into a right relationship with its god and preparing them for a joyous afterlife. Freemasonry's way of gaining salvation is in fact a way of losing salvation. If a man or woman trusts in their good works, whether Masonic, ritualistic, charitable, sacrificial, or otherwise, they are not trusting Christ's work on the cross. And anyone not trusting the cross, is lost.

6. OFFERS PURPORTEDLY DIVINE LIGHT. As already noted, Freemasonry's First Degree ritual teaches "light" is found only within Masonry. Therefore, all who are outside the Craft are in darkness. Its chief authorities interpret this "light" as primarily divine truth (from which also springs moral instruction). This exclusive divine light claim directly contradicts Christ's claims that He alone is and gives the light of divine truth: "*I am* the light of the world" (John 8:12). And because He, the living Word, indwells His written Word, the Bible, and He also indwells His people, the church, His (God's) Words "give light" (Psalm 119:130) and His church is "the light of the world" (Matthew 5:14). As shown earlier in this chapter, Christ's and Masonry's light claims cannot both be correct. One is offering the true light of divine truth and the other the false light of dark

deception—and being used by Lucifer, the first false "light bearer" who, to this day, disguises himself and his servants as "angel[s] of light" in this unbelieving, heretical, sin-darkened world (2 Corinthians 11:14-15).

7. MEETS IN A TEMPLE. Freemasons meet in buildings called "temples"—a term specifically describing religious structures in which Jews, Christians, or adherents of other faiths meet for religious worship and instruction. In the New Testament, "temple" is a metaphor for two things: Christ's body, the church (1 Corinthians 3:16-17), and individual Christians' bodies (1 Corinthians 6:19-20). Both these Christian "temples" are places where worship is offered and religious instruction received. The Heirloom Edition of the Masonic Bible states each Masonic lodge "represents some part of King Solomon's Temple."[17] Solomon's temple was a house of worship and center of religious instruction—*not* a center of mere philosophical, fraternal, social, or political instruction or activity. Therefore, like Solomon's temple, Masonic temples are houses of worship and centers of religious instruction.

8. CALLS ITS LODGE LEADERS "WORSHIPFUL MASTER." As described earlier, Masonic leaders' titles sound very religious. The local lodge leader's title is "Worshipful Master." Formerly, the word "worshipful" identified one as (a) distinguished, notable, or admirable. But today the word also connotes one is (b) a leader of religious worship or even (c) due reverential adoration (worship). I believe the first definition (a) is accurate. Why?

---

17. *The Holy Bible, Masonic Heirloom Edition*, 10.

Masons do not worship their lodge leaders. Nor is the Worshipful Master's primary duty to lead worship at every business meeting. However, it is not uncommon for lodges to occasionally host Masonic worship services that (in America or Great Britain) include singing Christian hymns. This overt Christian worship, alongside the Masonic altar, god, and claims of divine truth-light, confirms that Masonic temples are indeed centers of religious faith and practice.

9. Aims to mature men spiritually and morally. Freemasonry hopes to use its symbolic degree rituals to teach and cultivate "moral truths and doctrines" and "principles" intended to mature Masons spirituality and morality.[18] Inside most Masonic temples there are two square or rectangular stones prominently placed. One is a "rough ashlar," or stone freshly cut from the quarry, whose surface is uneven and in need of tooling. The other is a "perfect ashlar," or stone which is dressed (tooled with precision), smooth, and ready for use. These stones symbolize Masons, first as initiates entering the lodge with "rough cut" characters; and second, as mature Masons nearing the end of their lives, whose character flaws have been removed by obedience to Masonic teaching. Thus, they are better men, brothers, husbands, and fathers in this life and ready for placement in the Masonic temple (celestial lodge) in the next. Similar character development or formation is the aim of many religions. Christianity endeavors by the Holy Spirit's

---

18. Davenport, Reynolds, "Freemasonry Revealed: The Three Symbolic Degrees," North Carolina Grand Lodge Website, see https://www.grandlodge-nc.org/freemasonry-revealed (accessed 9/24/2024).

work, ministers' instructions, and the believer's obedience, to make the believer a perfect ashlar, "conformed to the image of his [God's] Son," Jesus (Romans 9:29; see Colossians 1:28). This makes the believer a better, or more fruitful, Christian in this life and ready for placement in Christ's temple (or kingdom) in the next. By thus pursuing the same goal of character transformation that other religions, especially Christianity, pursue, Freemasonry identifies itself as a religion.

10. Aspires to reform the world. For a secretive fraternity, Freemasonry is far more ambitious than one would expect. It plans to not only make good men better but also to eventually make this dysfunctional world perfect. By the good works and good teachings of its good men, Masonic luminaries envision bringing about a world order in which all religions see each other equally and, consequently, their adherents live together in idyllic peace. (More on this later in this chapter.) No surprise, this is the ultimate purpose of most religions—to change the world for good and ultimately bring in a golden age of righteousness, peace, and understanding under the rule of its deity. Christianity hopes to do the same after Christ returns to earth.

11. Uses Bible verses, symbols, and allusions to instruct. By using the Bible—the Christian religion's universally authoritative book—Freemasonry poses as a legitimate branch (denomination) of the Christian religion. It weaves biblical texts, symbols, and allusions into its instruction often. References to Solomon's temple are a favorite. The Phoenician architect who helped construct it, Hiram, is a central figure in Masonic lore.

Jesus' congratulatory words, "Well done, good and faithful servant," also appear frequently. The resurrection of the dead, and eternal life,[19] both biblical revelations, are spoken of multiple times. As stated earlier, the Great White Throne Judgment is prominently discussed, although it is interpreted incorrectly. And many other Bible links are made, openly or subtly. Why? As already noted, to ever so quietly and gradually convince the biblically untaught and spiritually undiscerning Mason he is receiving genuine Christian instruction. If Biblical symbols are used, the lessons drawn must be true, Christian, and safe. Not necessarily! The most dangerous heresies are not those using extrabiblical material but those using biblical texts and symbols that have been twisted to create false impressions. This is a hallmark of false religions ... and Freemasonry has this mark stamped indelibly upon it.

12. MIMICS, AND THUS RIVALS, THE CHURCH'S WORK. Freemasonry's plan to mature men spiritually and morally by its instruction parallels the church's work of progressively sanctifying believers (John 17:17; 1 Thessalonians 5:23-24). Its task of preparing its "good men made better" for eternal life and participation in its supposed "celestial lodge" parallels the church's work of preparing Christians to live, worship, and work in the eternal kingdom of God. Its invitation for Masons to enjoy a peaceful retreat with strife-free fellowship every time they visit the lodge parallels the sweet

---

19. Not every religion teaches all souls will consciously exist eternally. Seventh-Day Adventism teaches after the wicked are resurrected and judged, they will cease to exist (Annihilationism). See: https://www.adventist.org/death-and-resurrection/ (accessed 9/16/2024).

fellowship Christians enjoy whenever they gather with fellow Christians to worship, and learn and discuss the things of God. In these and other ways, the Masonic lodge mimics the church's calling and works. With one vital difference: Jesus and His redemption are ignored! Thus, Freemasonry not only rivals the church, if it could, it would replace it—despite the Craft's insistent claim that, when Christians become Masons, they become better Christians. Actually, the opposite is true: the more Christians pursue Masonic works, goals, teachings, and fellowship, the less they pursue their Christian equivalents. Unknowingly, then, the lodge represents Satan's perfect world: spiritually and morally mature men, great fellowship, good works, a peaceful world, all *without* Jesus!

Masons would have us believe their organization is merely another fraternal, civic, or service club designed for fellowship, influence, and charity. But this is clearly false. No mere fraternal, civic, or service organization—Civitans, Kiwanis, Rotary, Elks, Moose, and so forth—shares the twelve characteristics cited above. Such traits fall exclusively within the domain of religion.

Freemasonry's prominent sources agree. One of its most well-known nineteenth century authorities, Albert Pike, wrote:

> Every Masonic lodge is a temple of religion, and its teachings are instruction in religion.[20]
>
> —ALBERT PIKE

---

20. Carlson, Ron, Decker, Ed, *Fast Facts on False Teachings*, 80.

A colorful but controversial character, Pike (1809-1891) was a Confederate States Army general, author, poet, polymath, associate justice on the Arkansas Supreme Court, and Sovereign Grand Commander of the Supreme Council of the Scottish Rite Masons (Southern Jurisdiction). But he was also an outspoken racist, a good friend of Nathan Bedford, founder of the Ku Klux Klan and, at one time, the Klan's chief judicial officer.

Pike believed so firmly that Masonry is a viable religion that he performed a public "Masonic baptism" in New York City in 1865, in which six children were baptized by him with water and consecrated oil.[21] In an effort to distance themselves from Pike, some Masons today claim his views were not officially authorized by the Masonic lodge. Yet Pike is clearly held in high esteem as a Masonic philosopher by millions of Masons. His bust is proudly displayed (and earthly remains interred) in the prestigious House of the Temple of the Scottish Rite Southern Jurisdiction, in Washington, D.C. Since there is no definitive list of official American Masonic sources, Pike's opinions are clearly as authoritative as any other Masonic source, if not more. And Pike's quote above is clear: Freemasonry is a religion!

Masonic detractors also agree it is a religion. The prominent nineteenth century minister, Benjamin Titus Roberts (1823-1893) concluded:

> The god of the lodge is not the God of the Bible.
> —Rev. Benjamin Titus Roberts

---

21. Wikipedia, "Albert Pike," see: https://en.wikipedia.org/wiki/Albert_Pike (accessed 8/13/2024).

Blessed with penetrating, ultra-clear discernment, Roberts, the founder of the Free Methodist Church,[22] called Freemasonry "an alternate religion" and advised his congregation not to join or support it. Cain was the first to create an "alternate religion" (see Genesis 4:1-5) and the first to have his religion rejected by God. If Christianity reflects the true, God-directed worship of Abel, Freemasonry reflects the false, man-directed worship of Cain.

Everything about Freemasonry appeals to the "Cain" in us, our proud, independent, God-ignoring, fallen nature. In the "way of Cain" (Jude 11), or spirit of Cain's arrogance, Freemasonry suggests we ignore God's way of salvation and instead teach and practice salvation *our way!* It doesn't need a Savior, cross, or blood sacrifice, only its own bloodless sacrifices: good works guided by its own good teachings. Like Cain, Freemasonry is smugly confident God will receive, not reject, its proud offerings. One day it will see the light. The Bible says we need grace, faith, and the Lamb's redeeming work to be right with God. Meanwhile, Masonry persists in saying, we will do this thing our way, thank you, depending upon our goodness, meritorious works, and self-confidence. And with no Redeemer!

Summing up, Freemasonry unquestionably fits the Cambridge definition of a religion. It "believes in a god" and has a very well established "system of belief,"

---

22. The Free Methodist Church B.T. Roberts founded was based on, among other things, "freedom from secret societies." See: The Square Magazine, "Freemasonry," see https://www.thesquaremagazine.com/mag/freemasonry/ (accessed 6/27/2024).

if not "worship." Thus, it is a religion, though a false one! It is "Cainish," a humanly contrived religion cleverly designed to mimic, rival, even replace the God-ordained religion of Christianity. Therefore, it is not, as Masons claim, a compliment to Christianity. It is its competitor. And as with Cain's religion, God unequivocally rejects it.

FREEMASONRY'S VISION: WORLD TRANSFORMATION!

Joseph Ford Newton, introduced in Chapter 1, asserted Masonry's loftiest aim is ... to change the world! Yes, he openly cast the vision that Masons are building not only better men but also a better society, and ultimately, a universal brotherhood of men and religion. Or, in his words, "to bring about a universal league of mankind and to form mankind into a great redemptive brotherhood."[23] Since Masonry requires only belief in a god, but *not* Jesus, the "great redemptive brotherhood" Newton envisions is a universal Masonic brotherhood that redeems mankind and embraces all religions and gods. Without Jesus and His emphatic claim that He is the only way to the Father (John 14:6)!

Newton's statement is surprising since he was originally ordained a Baptist pastor. He surely knew John 14:6. Yet he wrote often of a brotherhood of men or "brotherhood of the world"[24] which included the *unredeemed* populace. His publisher spotlighted Newton's chief message: "Throughout his entire ministry [he] strove

---

23. Carlson, Ron, Decker, Ed, *Fast Facts on False Teachings*, 78.

24. Newton, Joseph Ford, *The Builders*, vii.

to promote a brotherhood of religion" and his "lifelong sermon" was:

> We can never have a *religion of brotherhood* on earth until we have a *brotherhood of religion*.[25]
> —JOSEPH FORD NEWTON

Though an ordained Christian minister, Newton denies that a "religion of brotherhood on earth" has already come. Yet it has: Christianity! Therefore, his hope anticipates the coming of *another* worldwide "religion of brotherhood" once mankind has successfully created a worldwide "brotherhood of religion[s]." Clearly, to him, Freemasonry *is* this "brotherhood of religion[s]" destined to bring about a utopian brotherhood of men worldwide.

Pause and ponder just how unbiblical his vision is. The peaceful joining of all the world's deeply contradictory and inherently adversarial religions? Each promoting its own unique chief deity and incompatible doctrines? We may as well claim that Jesus and Lucifer will get together! Or that Jezebel and her Baal worship will unite blissfully with Elijah and the worship of Yahweh. Or that Islamic Jihadists will abandon their Quranic doctrine of killing insubmissive infidels and begin gently loving Jews and embracing Christians! Like these, Newton's envisioned unity is totally unbiblical, patently unreal, and farcical. Cannot, will not, happen! However long and earnestly Newton's Masonic disciples hope for it.

Newton's experience helps us understand his vision.

---

25. Ibid, the Frontispiece.

After serving the Baptist church, he pastored several other churches and ultimately converted to the Unitarian Universalist church. This heretical sect rejects the Trinity and believes in universal reconciliation, which teaches all people, including Judas, and even Satan, will ultimately be saved and spend eternity with God. It also affirms that all faiths, not just Christianity, possess divine truth we should learn and live by. Newton's body of work shows he believed this embracing of all faiths and their doctrines will lead to the "brotherhood of religion[s]"—or a universal religion comprised of all religions. And Freemasonry playing a key role!

Newton believed Freemasonry is destined to build[26] a "brotherhood of religion[s]" despite those religions' radically opposed core beliefs. Every honest rational person, however gentle, loving, and magnanimous, recognizes it is impossible for all religions, while contradicting each other on the identity of God and the way of salvation, to truly become one. Why? They are not one. They are radically diverse! Far from being brothers, they are spiritual *enemies*, doing mortal doctrinal combat daily to lay claim to men's eternal souls. That is, if they truly believe the widely disparate beliefs they profess.

So, while Newton yearns to build a religion fusing all religions, Jesus asserts He is the exclusive "way" to salvation and "no man" can come to the Father but by *Him* (John 14:6). And He and Newton cannot both be correct.

---

26. Thus, the title of Newton's primary work, *The Builders*.

Not surprisingly, Newton also claimed that, like the church, Masonry contains divine life:

> More than an institution, more than a tradition, more than a society, Masonry is one of the forms of the *Divine Life upon earth* ... a great historic fellowship of the seekers and finders of God ... a center of moral and spiritual power.[27]

Newton's insistence that Masonry contains divine life, helps seekers find God, and is a center of moral and spiritual power, shows us clearly that, in his mind, it is Christianity's equal. Or replacement! His claim that Masonry is "one of the forms" of divine life on earth further implies there are multiple repositories of divine life on earth. This suggests other faiths (Judaism, Islam, Sikhism, Mormonism, the Watchtower Society, and so forth) also hold divine life. Yet the Bible makes it clear that the church and true Christianity *alone* offer genuine divine life and the path to eternal salvation. And no other entity or religion does so. Certainly not a fraternal secret society whose teachings are built on acknowledged myths.

Summing up, Newton held that all religions are viable ways to God and offer divine truth, life, salvation, and spiritual maturity. He was convinced Masonry, not Christianity, would bring about a worldwide "brotherhood of religions" and, subsequently, a worldwide "religion of brotherhood." This same deadly heresy will be taught by the coming one-world church. During its short tenure, it will gather all religions under its dark

---

27. Newton, Joseph Ford, *The Builders*, 235, 236, 239.

wings and ultimately offer all followers of all faiths as a living sacrifice to Antichrist, the Satan-indwelt "man of sin" who will "exalt himself above all that is called God, or that is worshiped, so that he, as God, sitteth in the temple of God, showing himself that he is God" (2 Thessalonians 2:3-4). Thus, we conclude, Newton's vision is of the antichrist spirit. It is satanic. The apostle John anticipated this antichrist spirit working in this church age: "This is the spirit of antichrist, which you have heard was coming, and is now already in the world" (1 John 4:3, NKJV). Freemasonry is one of its manifestations.

FREEMASONRY'S REMNANTS OF RACISM

American Freemasonry began as an all-white men's secret society during the height of eighteenth-century slavery. The writings of some of its nineteenth-century officers reveal they unquestionably held racist views and, as previously noted, at least one major figure, Albert Pike, was a leading member of the Ku Klux Klan.

Nevertheless, some progress was made. The first men of color entered the American lodges in the 1770s. Subsequently, Masonic lodges were founded in several black African nations and began spreading to others. Meanwhile, many Masonic lodges in America have since accepted African Americans. But not all. American Freemasonry today remains largely though not entirely segregated, with separate black (Prince Hall) lodges and white lodges. Mainstream Freemasons today refer to the black lodges as "parallel" Masonic organizations, carefully avoiding the more-accurate, less-flattering adjective, "segregated." As of 2011, nine primarily southern states still did not recognize Prince Hall members as true Masons.[28]

This remnant of American racial segregation is a clear contradiction of Freemasonry's lofty ideals of the brotherhood of all men and its professed quest to forge a truly universal brotherhood. It also contradicts the standard of the Masonic Bible upon which its members swear their oaths, which states seven times God is "no respecter of persons" (Acts 10:34),[29] or "shows no partiality" (ESV), but rather accepts true worshipers from "every nation" (Acts 10:35). It further ignores the "fundamentals of Masonry which claim for man the threefold heritage of Liberty, Equality, and Fraternity."[30] And, finally, it contradicts the lofty universal racial unity advocated by Joseph Ford Newton, who, in his 1948 classic book, *The Builders*, lamented:

> Still there is racial rancor [in the world]—a thing slithered with blood and black with bitterness; still there is a religious bigotry which blasphemes the genius of brotherhood. For such things [racial and religious division] there is no place in this our Brotherhood.[31]

---

28. They are: Alabama, Georgia, Tennessee, Mississippi, Arkansas, South Carolina, West Virginia, Florida, and Louisiana. This information is, of course, subject to change. See: https://themasonslady.com/category/freemasonry-101/ (accessed 9/20/2024).

29. Deuteronomy 10:17; 2 Chronicles 19:7; Acts 10:34-35; Romans 2:11; Ephesians 6:9; Colossians 3:25; 1 Peter 1:17.

30. *The Holy Bible, Heirloom Family Edition*, "The Internal Workings of Freemasonry: Blue Lodge Masonry, The Fellow-Craft Degree," 11.

31. Newton, Joseph Ford, *The Builders*, xv.

Yet, nearly ninety years after Newton penned this, racial division still lingers in the "Brotherhood." The segregated lodges apparently must interpret Newton's words as advocating the "genius of brotherhood" of all men *except* African Americans.[32]

FREEMASONRY'S BLOOD OATHS

Freemasonry's degree rituals require initiates swear a blood oath that they will not disclose the secrets of the Craft. A blood oath is a vow to suffer capital punishment if unfaithful to one's pledge. Here Masons have no plausible defense. No cleverly packaged presentation can make a blood oath appear to be normal, rational, or admirable. From every perspective it is abnormal, irrational, and deplorable. And certainly not Christian. If the oath was merely a pledge to do one's utmost to not disclose the secrets of Freemasonry, that would be defensible. But when the self-imposed penalty of death for such disclosures is included, it exposes the true pagan, unscriptural, and un-Christlike spirit behind Freemasonry. Masons get around this by claiming the gruesome physical penalties described in its blood oaths are retained merely for their *allegorical* meaning. If so, why use them at all? Why not amend the ritual wordings to use more reasonable allegorical language?

The blood oaths used in the first three degrees are simply terrifying:

---

32. And in saying this, I am *not* advocating for twenty-first century American wokeism, which, at base, promotes reverse racism by advocating that *the entire race* of their typical racist antagonists is uniformly and incorrigibly racist.

Looking Deeper: Examining Freemasonry's Core Heresies

Entered Apprentice Degree

Binding myself under no less a penalty than having my throat cut across, my tongue torn out by its roots, and buried in the rough sands of the sea ...

Fellowcraft Degree

Binding myself under no less a penalty than that of having my left breast torn open, my heart plucked out and given as prey to the wild beasts of the fields and the fowls of the air ...

Master Mason Degree

Binding myself under no less a penalty than that of having my body severed in twain, my bowels taken from thence and burned in ashes ...[33]

In the Old Testament, making oaths to God was permitted, on one condition: those making them should do so only after solemnly determining they could, and would, faithfully fulfill them. To make oaths or vows to God frivolously, or neglect fulfilling them, was sin, and punishable by God:

> When you make a promise to God, don't delay in following through, for God takes no pleasure in fools. Keep all the promises you make to him. It is better to say nothing than to make a promise and not keep it. Don't let your mouth make you sin.
> —Ecclesiastes 5:4-6, NLT

If this is God's command regarding oaths or pledges

---

33. Carlson, Ron, Decker, Ed, *Fast Facts on False Teachings*, 75.

made to Him, it follows that making solemn vows (oaths, affirmations, pledges) to men or organizations frivolously or unfaithfully is also considered sin today. "But Christians are under the New Covenant now," you may respond.

Yes, but the New Testament goes even further, forbidding *all* oath-taking: "Do not take an oath at all" (Matthew 5:33, ESV; see James 5:12). Therefore, how much more does God deplore pagan blood oaths! Aware of this, Freemasonry very carefully hides its blood oaths from the public. And when Masons do speak of them, they euphemize them as mere "solemn pledges" or "obligations" to be kept "inviolate[ly]."

Describing the Entered Apprentice Degree ritual, *The Heirloom Masonic Bible* states:

> The Apprentice is entrusted with certain secrets of the Order ... and is *pledged* to "keep counsel of all things spoken in Lodge or chamber by any Masons ... He is invested with certain "Secrets," which, of course, he must keep *inviolate*.[34]

For those undergoing the second, or Fellowcraft, Degree, it states:

> The *pledge to secrecy* with reference to the internal workings of the Institution is broadened and strongly re-enforced ... The endowments and investitures of the Order given in this Degree are to be

---

34. *The Holy Bible, Heirloom Family Edition,* "The Internal Workings of Freemasonry: Blue Lodge Masonry, The Entered Apprentice Degree," 10.

guarded with *inviolate fidelity* and obedience to the tenets and laws of Masonry are exacted with *great emphasis*.[35]

The essence of these blood oaths is *loyalty to the death* for one's Masonic trusts, alliances, and beliefs. This, too, should alert Christians for at least two reasons. First, shouldn't a Christian's first allegiance be to *Jesus*, for whom he (or she) is willing to die a martyr rather than deny the Lord's name or Word, and to no other person or entity? Second, shouldn't his next loyalty be to his fellow Christians, who he is obligated to love as sacrificially as Christ has loved him (John 13:34-35), and not to Masons or any others outside the body of Christ? To instead solemnly pledge utter loyalty to Freemasons and their secrets is a perversion of Christian loyalty. No Christian should ever pledge loyalty, much less to the death, to a neo-pagan, cultish secret society.

FREEMASONRY'S LINK TO SHRINERS—AND ISLAM!

The Shriners organization, originally the "Ancient Arabic Order of the Nobles of the Mystic Shrine," now simply "Shriners International," was formed expressly for fun, fellowship, and philanthropy. All Shriners must first be Master (3rd Degree) Masons.

Shriners' public image is an attractive mixture of comedy, entertainment, and charity. They frequently participate in parades with their colorful costumes and midget "funny" cars. Since 1906, the Shrine Circus has entertained people in cities across America and Canada.

---

35. Ibid, 11.

Most well-known, however, are the Shriners Hospitals for children (Shriners Children's) which, since 1922 have given medical care to great numbers of children. Today (2024) Shriners International has 22 hospitals in the United States, Canada, and Mexico. Since Shriners must also be Masons, the two fraternal orders are integrally linked.

Below is the concise history of the Shriners International taken directly from its official website:

> In 1870, a group of 13 Masons would regularly meet at the Knickerbocker Cottage in New York City. Often, discussion turned to forming a new fraternity for Masons, based on the tenets of Freemasonry but with the added elements of fun and fellowship.
>
> Walter Fleming, M.D., and Billy Florence, an actor, were among the members of the group. Florence had been on tour in Europe and attended a party given by an Arabian diplomat. The exotic style, flavors and music of the Arabian-themed party led Florence to suggest this as the theme of the new fraternity, while Dr. Fleming and other members of the group then drafted the ritual, designed the emblem and costumes, formulated a salutation and declared that members would wear the red fez. The name of this new fraternity was the Ancient Arabic Order of the Nobles of the Mystic Shrine.
>
> While the fraternity's first official meeting was in 1871 at the Knickerbocker Cottage, a meeting in 1872 established the first chapter, Mecca Shriners,

on September 26. Today, there are more than 195 chapters in countries around the world.[36]

This public image seems solidly good and the benevolent Shriners hospitals are especially commendable. But there are some crucial darker facts the Shriners International site does not disclose.

Shriners' Fezzes

Shriners' distinctive red caps, or "fezzes," prominently display the Islamic sword and crescent. Immediately this links them symbolically with the false religion of Islam. But the connection goes deeper. The fez's red color represents a macabre historical fact that is an honor to Muslims, a mockery of Christians, and a deep offense to Christ.

In the eighth century, invading Muslims slaughtered 50,000 Christians in Fez, Morocco, while fanatically shouting the first pillar of Islam, "There is no god but Allah and Mohammed is his prophet." During this horrific massacre, the Muslims purportedly dipped their fez-shaped hats in the blood of the Christians, and thus dark, or blood, red became their distinctive color. Centuries later, the Shriners, to further their new fraternity's association with Arab culture, adopted the red fez as their official headwear. No true Christian informed of the fez's history would dare proudly wear such a symbol of violent Islamic conquest and the shameful slaughter of innocent Christians.

---

36. "Our History: 150 Years of Fun and Fellowship," see: https://www.shrinersinternational.org/en/who-we-are/history-of-the-fraternity (accessed 9/9/2024).

It is as unthinkable as Jews proudly embroidering their coats with Swastikas. Or African Americans celebrating black history month by wearing yokes or nooses. Or eastern Europeans who suffered brutal oppression under the Soviets joyfully parading around with large placards bearing Stalin's image. Or Christians proudly wearing Roman togas boldly embroidered with the name of Nero, who falsely blamed and executed thousands of Christians for the fire of Rome (A.D. 64), even inhumanly burning some as human torches to light his gardens. Some may scoff at this objection, claiming most Shriners do not know the history of the fez. My response is, why not? It's public knowledge. Shouldn't they understand the symbolism of their own regalia? If their poor choice of hats truly stems from ignorance, let them show it by changing their headwear. If not, I say, shame on the Shriners—who are also Masons! But they have another, far worse reason to be ashamed.

Submission to Allah— and Alliance with Jihadists!

When a Mason is initiated as a Shriner, during the ceremony he is required to bow at the Shriner's Altar of Obligation. There, with hands tied behind his back, he professes that Allah is the "god of his fathers."[37] Though hard to believe, this is nevertheless true. Even a novice Christian with little or no biblical knowledge knows intuitively that bowing to a false god is idolatry. Perhaps some Christians are so ignorant as to think the god of Islam is also the God of Christianity. But that is not

---

37. Carlson, Ron, Decker, Ed, *Fast Facts on False Teachings*, 72.

Looking Deeper: Examining Freemasonry's Core Heresies

true. So, an initiate's very first act as a Shriner is a grave sin and an abomination to the only true God. And there is more.

The god of Islam does not exist. "Allah" is actually a demonic entity posing as a deity who deceives and oppresses the millions who serve him. When a Mason submits to Allah in his Shriners initiation, he is effectively becoming a Muslim, because "Islam" is derived from an Arabic word (*islām*) meaning "submission," or "surrender." Or, more specifically, submission to the will of Allah. By confessing Allah is his father's god, the Shriner unwittingly opens his whole being and family to Islam's dark demonic covering and harmful influence. This is inexcusable. Every Christian alive today should recognize the terrible grief Islam has caused the world in the name of Allah.

Islam's religious oppression campaign began with its first significant enlargement in the seventh and eighth centuries from the Arabian peninsula to the Middle East, North Africa, and Spain. All this growth outside Arabia came almost exclusively by not peaceful evangelism but bloody conquests and coercive conversions. Mohammed was a man of blood, leading numerous plundering raids on caravans, commanding large military assaults, and personally killing hundreds with his own sword. Mohammed's religion reflects his violence—despite the Quran's calls for justice and peace. Of all the world's religions, Islam is the *only* one that justifies bloodshed in the "defense" of its faith against "infidels." When in the Middle Ages ignorant Christians followed deceived popes in the false hope of salvation by participation in the Crusades, it was the result of grossly misunderstanding the teachings of Christ and the New Testament. Christ not only taught peace, He lived it. Rather than killing with the sword, like Mohammed, Jesus meekly died by it to do His Father's will and save all who believe on Him. But when Muslims pursue holy war, they do so in full compliance with their founder's well-documented personal experience and one of his religion's most fundamental teachings: Jihad![38]

In the seventh century, Mohammed first presented his professed divine revelations to Jews and Christians, presenting himself as a prophet to the Jews and apostle to the Christians. Both groups saw through his deceptions and rejected him. Deeply incensed, Mohammed, a vengeful man, soon developed a bitter hatred for Jews and Christians. It is not surprising, therefore, that those who follow Mohammed today share his penchant for violence, vengefulness, and deep antipathy for Jews and Christians.

---

38. Jihad (lit., *struggle*, especially "in the way of God") is a central doctrine of Islam (formerly one of its pillars) and considered a duty by devout Muslims worldwide. It takes at least three forms: (1) struggling against one's inner sins, (2) struggling for Islam with the tongue or pen, and (3) struggling violently against the enemies of Islam to defend or spread the faith (by holy war; or for many, by terrorism). Christianity also encourages its faithful to "struggle" to defend or increase the faith. But we do so: (1) by putting off sin and walking closely with Christ as His living sacrifices and witnesses to this lost world, (2) by faithfully exercising our spiritual gifts and pursuing our divinely appointed ministries, (3) by personally, ministerially, or missionally evangelizing the lost, and (4) by training disciples, who then also become Christ's witnesses and spread His gospel. But Christ's example and teachings *never* authorize us to "struggle" violently to spread our faith. On Jihad, see Wikipedia: https://en.wikipedia.org/wiki/Jihad (accessed 9/09/24).

Pause and think of all the grief Islam has caused and is still causing. Offensive wars launched for Allah's honor killed hundreds of thousands when Muslim Caliph-led forces conquered the Middle East, Egypt, northern Africa, and Spain from the eighth to the fifteenth centuries. Those targeted were largely Christian populations. And since the State of Israel was restored in 1948, its Jewish citizens have been relentlessly targeted by Islamic armies or terrorists, all in the name of Jihad,[39] while shouting mesmerically, "Allahu akbar" (Allah is the greatest) and "Death to the Jews." America's 9/11 attacks were also the work of Jihadists. And for many decades the whole world has been vexed by Islamic zealots seeking to blow up buildings, hijack airplanes, bomb shopping malls, and even randomly slash pedestrians' throats, all to "defend" Islam from the infidels and, in their demented minds, bring glory to Allah.

The latest major Jihadist incident was Hamas' invasion of Israel October 7, 2023. During this unprovoked attack, Hamas terrorists raped, maimed, beheaded, and

---

39. They see their actions as honorable. They are "defending" the Islamic faith by defending the Islamic Palestinians against the Zionist Jews who have occupied "their" land. But the truth is this: the so-called "Palestinians" are *not* the indigenous people of Palestine. They are rather Arabs who migrated there from the surrounding nations of Egypt, Jordan, Syria, Lebanon, and Iraq. Thus, "their" land is indeed in the Middle East, but it is in Egypt, Jordan, Syria, Lebanon, and Iraq. Not Israel. The Jews' claim to their homeland points back to God's ancient land grant repeatedly recorded in the Bible (Exodus 3:16-17; 6:6-8; 23:23-31). Therefore, in relocating to Palestine and reestablishing a Jewish State in 1948, the Jewish people were merely repossessing what God sovereignly gave them centuries ago and what was taken from them by force when the Romans conquered and expelled them in the 1st and 2nd centuries A.D.

desecrated Jews and others at will, killing 1,200 innocent Israeli men, women, and babies, and taking 251 hostages. Why? They were under the demonic inspiration of decades of virulent Palestinian propaganda and centuries of Jihadist doctrine. While I acknowledge, yes, there are millions of moderate Muslims worldwide who don't embrace Jihad, and may not even know their religion's violent history, I also assert there are millions more who do know its history and fully embrace and ardently practice Jihad. While sophisticated Islamic apologists feverishly try to distance this blatantly murderous madness from "true Islam," it is actually the *real*, original, and historic Islam as practiced by Mohammed and his Caliphs. No mere minor teaching, Jihad is rooted in Islam's holy books, the Quran and Hadith, making it a fundamental, vital, and indispensable tenet of Islam. And in many countries Jihad is still being drilled into the minds of millions of children daily, who are growing up hoping they, too, will one day have a chance to wage one or another form of holy war in "defense" of Islam, especially against Jews and Christians (particularly Americans).

Knowing this history, and current events, how could any Christian wear a Shriners' fez emblazoned with two overtly Islamic symbols, the Islamic sword (scimitar) and crescent moon? How could he thus ally himself with Islamists driven by a blood lust to wage Jihad against Jews and Christians? And how could he profess in a most solemn initiation ceremony that Allah, the demonic god ruling Muslims worldwide, is "his father's god" and, by extension, his own?

Chapter Four

LOOKING THROUGH: PENETRATING FREEMASONRY'S FAÇADE

HAVING LOOKED DEEPLY INTO the dark heart of Freemasonry and discovered its core heresies, we have one final investigative duty to perform. Well aware of the unappealing truths we discussed in Chapter 3, Masons have cleverly constructed a false front, a façade of appealing selling points to put forward to the public. Its purpose is obvious: to hide the Craft's unappealing core beliefs. We will briefly describe these selling points so they will not deceive us into thinking they are the weightier facts and Freemasonry's heresies the lighter. They are: "Enjoy good fellowship!" "Become more influential!" "Participate in good works!" "Enjoy the help of fellow Masons!" "Become a better man!" and "Join the ranks of history's great Masons!"

FREEMASONRY'S SELLING POINTS

The following are the primary talking points Masons use to build their public image and motivate men to seek membership in their lodges. In the interests of fairness, I acknowledge that all these selling points are genuinely good. I will make no attempt to present them as being bad or harmful in and of themselves.

"Enjoy Good Fellowship!"

Masons frequently say one of their main aims is to enjoy wonderful fraternal fellowship. They retreat from this politically, socially, and religiously contentious world to quietly enjoy common interests with other like-minded good men in the local lodge. To preserve this ideal unity, they forbid that any Mason advocate or argue his political or religious opinions, or try to convert another Mason to his preferred religion and its teachings. By doing so, they sell the local lodge as a haven or refuge from the relentless furor of life. This claim is true, as Masons do enjoy their harmonious lodge fellowship.

"Become More Influential!"

Masons also attract interest in their organization by telling inquirers that by building relationships with more experienced and influential Masons, younger Masons grow to become more influential in their chosen fields, professions, cities, and nations. This is often true. Many Masons enjoy above-average influence in their communities, thanks to the favors, introductions, compliments, endorsements, and open doors offered by fellow Masons.

"Participate in Good Works!"

Charitable works are another stated attraction. Masonic lodges support The Red Cross, The Masonic Charitable Foundation, The Teddies for Loving Care, Masonic Homes (for elderly Masons), the Masonic Model Student Assistance Program, and many other beneficial local and statewide charities. Shriners, who are also Masons, are also well known for their charitable works, especially their children's hospitals (Shriners Children's). There is everything commendable and nothing condemnable about these endeavors. Our world needs more good works and less bad.

"Enjoy the Help of Fellow Masons!"

Another oft-mentioned appeal is that Masons go to great lengths to help fellow Masons in distress or trouble, with brotherly counsel, financial aid, physical labor, and other means of timely assistance. They even help Masons who are in trouble with the law—except in cases of murder or treason. And they make good on this claim. Here, again, I find only good. Christians might learn a lesson from Masons in this regard. Jesus commended the Samaritan who went out of his way, and his prejudices, to help a wounded Jew by the roadside (Luke 11:30-37). And what Jesus commends, I dare not criticize, much less condemn.

"Become a Better Man!"

Masons' primary good work, as stated repeatedly by Masons and this book, is making good men better—better husbands, fathers, brothers, workers, and friends. How? By receiving idealistic Masonic teaching and putting it into practice in their daily lives. Masons claim, when acted upon, their ethical code and its principles facilitate personal spiritual growth and moral development, and provide crucial guidance through the confusing maze of life. Strictly speaking, there is nothing wrong with Masons studying and practicing ideals for better living. While it is impossible for Masonic teaching alone to foster true spiritual and moral maturity and impart flawless life guidance (only the Bible and Holy Spirit do this, and only for born-again Christians), it is on balance more helpful than harmful. In our ever more shockingly immoral world, any source advocating for morality is better than none. This, too, falls squarely into the category of good.

"Join the Ranks of History's Great Masons!"

Freemasonry boasts a long and prestigious list of famous past Masons. And their claim is neither false nor insignificant.

No less than fifteen US Presidents have been members of Masonic lodges. They are: George Washington, James Monroe, Andrew Jackson, James K. Polk, James Buchanan, Andrew Johnson, James A. Garfield, William McKinley, Theodore Roosevelt, William H. Taft, Warren G. Harding, Franklin D. Roosevelt, Harry Truman, Lyndon B. Johnson, and Gerald A. Ford. Of these, George Washington is especially venerated. Portraits of Washington are found in almost every lodge throughout America. His likeness even appears prominently in the opening pages of the primary Masonic Bible, *The Heirloom Family Bible*.

Freemasonry experienced significant growth in America during the eighteenth century. Consequently, many of America's founding fathers were Masons, such as, Benjamin Franklin, John Handcock, Paul Revere, and John Marshall. It is estimated that nine of the fifty-six signers of the Declaration of Independence were Masons and thirteen of the thirty-nine who signed the U.S. Constitution. Numerous Senators and Congressmen have since been or are now members of the Craft. Pierre Charles L'Enfant, designer of Washington, D.C., wore the Masonic apron, as did Benjamin Henry Latrobe, architect of the original U.S. Capitol. Masons laid the cornerstones of many of the original government buildings in Washington, D.C. Masonic emblems and designs still dot the city. Nineteenth Century Masons include the famous Samuel Clemens (Mark Twain) and infamous John Brown. Many famous twentieth-century figures from various walks of life were Masons: Walt Disney, Louis B. Mayer, Cecile B. DeMille, Will Rogers, J. Edgar Hoover, Douglas MacArthur, John Wayne (Marion Robert Morrison), Sam Ervin, Earl Warren, John Glenn, and Arnold Palmer, to name a few.[1]

Many famous foreigners were also Masons, including musical giants, Wolfgang A. Mozart and Franz Joseph Haydn. Even the great Sir Winston Churchill joined the English Masonic Lodge when he was a young man, apparently because his fathers had done so, but later withdrew and did not advance further in the Masonic degrees.[2]

---

1. Business Insider India Online Magazine, "17 of The Most Influential Masons Ever," (July 26, 2021), See: https://www.businessinsider.in/politics/17-of-the-most-influential-freemasons-ever/slidelist/32376628.cms#slideid=32376639#slideid=32376634 (accessed 10/22/2024).

2. "Winston Churchill was initiated as a young man [age 26, 1901] but never progressed in the order and has taken no part for many years," Sir Sydney White, Grand Secretary, United Grand Lodge of England (1937-1957), from "Seven Facts about Freemason Winston Churchill," see: https://masonicfind.com/masonic-facts-winston-churchill (accessed 6/24/24).

This is a very impressive list indeed that few, if any, fraternal or service organizations, religious or irreligious, can equal. As with the Masons' previous selling points, this one also is true. And it is most appealing. But the appeal is to our base human pride, not to the humility Christ has placed in our redeemed hearts, which are driven now with the highest motive of pleasing Him—who by His life example and Word teaches us to not foster or serve but *abandon* the "pride of life" (Matthew 23:12; Philippians 2:5-8; James 4:6, 10; 1 John 2:15-17).

From the viewpoint of the natural, unregenerated heart, though, who wouldn't fancy the idea that, by joining the celebrated company of luminaries named above, one was standing shoulder to shoulder with greatness? And perhaps destined for the same?[3]

SUMMING UP THE SELLING POINTS

Having established that Freemasonry's selling points are not only valid but also good, the burden is now on me to show why these appealing elements are outweighed on the scales of judgment by Freemasonry's heresies.

All Freemasonry's selling points create an effective psychological and moral allurement. Hearing them, men want to become Masons. When we challenge this by the many counterclaims presented in this book, two powerful unspoken questions arise in men's (and women's) minds. First, how could so many good things be so bad? Second, how could so many great men be so

---

3. Some famous Masons today are: Jesse Jackson, Steve Wozniak, Buzz Aldrin, John Elway, and Shaquille O'Neal.

wrong? These quiet, internal questions demand clear, well-reasoned explanations. Here is my case.

#1 - *How Could So Many Good Things Be So Bad?*

The good is the enemy of the best, because it lures people to accept less than the best. In themselves, good things are never bad—or they would not be good in the first place! But good things become bad when they are intentionally used to hide something evil and harmful, luring men to accept less than the best so they will never discover the best. In this case, Freemasonry, which we have already proven to be a religion, is the good and Christianity the best.

When we probe deeper, as we have done in this book, and penetrate Freemasonry's alluring façade of good works and great men, we discover that what candidates for Masonry are told is not the problem. The problem is what they are *not* told. These omissions are crucial. And profoundly, even eternally, harmful. Masonry's selling points benefit Masons in this brief, transitory life; its heresies, if believed, will harm them forever.

For instance, Masonic candidates are *not* informed that Masonry teaches a false gospel, with a false pathway to salvation and heaven, and that this brings them under the grave, biblical anathema of the apostle Paul (Galatians 1:7-9). More specifically, they are *not* told that Masonic teaching promises eternal life to all Masons who faithfully live by Masonic teaching. Yet Jesus famously taught we "must" receive Him and His redemption by experiencing a radical change of heart that comes only as we repent of our sins (Matthew 4:17) and receive a life-changing spiritual rebirth (John 3:3-8).

And, as covered earlier, Masons are told the single most important requirement of the lodge is that they believe in a god, or supreme being.[4] But they are *not* told that such faith has no saving merit. Masons may easily think it does, since they are taught that, with such faith, they may then work their way to heaven by faithfully obeying Masonic teaching during their lifetime. Millions of sinners are in hell today who in life believed in a higher being, but never accepted the way of salvation offered by the one true God through His Son's sacrificial death. James says even condemned demons in hell have faith in a higher being: "You say you have faith, for you believe that there is one God. Good for you! Even the demons believe this, and they tremble in terror" (James 2:19, NLT). It is personal belief in a personal Savior, Jesus, that saves, not vague mental assent to the idea of a supreme being.

Masons are promised that over the course of their lives Masonic teaching will lead them to become spiritually and morally mature, transformed from rough-cut ashlar stones into perfect ashlars, ready to take their place in the eternal, heavenly temple, or "celestial lodge" in Masonic jargon. But they are *not* told this work of sanctification and spiritual formation is impossible unless they receive Christ's new-birth experience, and subsequently receive the Holy Spirit, seek Christ personally every day, study the Bible diligently, obey it faithfully, apply their minister's biblical teaching and counsel to their lives, and obey the Holy Spirit's crucial corrections and guidance.

---

4. Chapters 2 and 3 discuss this.

Masons are encouraged to seek the fellowship of fellow Masons in the lodge. Yet they are *not* told they should seek edifying spiritual fellowship where Christ has already sovereignly provided it: with born-again Christian men and women in their local churches, and with true Christians everywhere, and that Christian fellowship was, and still is, a primary pillar of New Testament church life (Acts 2:42, 46). Masonic fellowship, however good, is not Christian fellowship. The former is natural and relaxing, the latter is spiritual and deeply strengthening. The former may relieve the nerves, but the latter revives the soul.

In all these ways, Masonic good blocks men from seeing and seeking Christ's best. In a very real sense, Masonry *replaces* Christianity. The Masonic gospel replaces Christ's gospel. Masonic teaching replaces Christian instruction. Memorizing Masonic degrees and lectures replaces memorizing Bible verses and stories. Masonic good works replace the "good works" God has foreordained we walk in in Christ (Ephesians 2:10). Glorying in great Masons replaces admiring faithful biblical overcomers. Masonic fellowship replaces Christian fellowship. Men make the lodge their spiritual and moral growth center instead of the church. This is the heart of my objections ... and Satan's object.

He plans to use Masonry to draw Christians, and potential Christian converts, away from the true gospel, biblical teaching, Christian fellowship, pursuing Christian good works, emulating biblical overcomers, and a Christ- and church-centered lifestyle. Or, to keep Christians from *going on to fully know Christ* by walking in the rich spiritual and natural provisions He has wisely and lovingly provided for us for our highest good.

For example, when non-Christian Masons are troubled about their soul and sin, they will hope for salvation in the Masonic gospel rather than Christ's gospel. They will think faithfulness to Masonic code is the way to God and blissful eternal life when Jesus plainly said *He* is the only Way to the Father and salvation, and there is no other (John 10:7-9; 14:6).

When in adversity, Masons will look for the help of fellow Masons, rather than the help of praying, loving Christian brothers and sisters in their local church. Thus, they become more emotionally attached to the Masonic fraternity than to their Christian brothers. Time and again, when trouble strikes, they turn to the Craft and its fraternity instead of Christ and the ecclesiastical brotherhood.

When Masons face spiritual or moral questions in life, they will look to their Masonic instruction rather than Christian teaching, and trust in the fallible humanistic wisdom of Masonic philosophers and local Masons rather than the infallible wisdom of Scripture and sure guidance of Spirit-led Christian counselors.

In these and other ways, Masonry is a dangerous, obstinate competitor to Christianity, a diabolically false man-made church specifically designed to supplant the divinely created ekklēsia. Its beliefs and doctrines are founded on the tragically false humanistic assumption that man is basically good and can redeem his faults by faithfully keeping an upright moral code. Yet this doctrine ignores the real facts: man is incorrigibly corrupt and lost in his fallen state and must have a Savior to redeem him. And once spiritually reborn, redeemed Christians will grow into personal spiritual and moral maturity only by faithfulness to Christ's biblical teaching, obedience to the instruction of godly ministers, openness to the quiet inner counsel of the Holy Spirit, and successfully enduring their God-ordained tests.

Summing up, Masonry is at its core the worship of Cain pitting itself against the worship of Abel all over again. But this time, the deadly struggle is being played out on a worldwide scale! Masonry presents a naturally attractive man-approved system of religion designed to make the only God-approved religion unnecessary. Thus, Masonry seeks to *usurp* the place and duties of the Redeemer and His church in men's lives. Its good prevents men from experiencing Christ's best. It claims to offer true light yet truly delivers only darkness. It produces a thick smokescreen of human spirituality and morality that keeps men's eyes from seeing the divine spirituality and morality in Christ. And we will never discover and walk in what we cannot see.

These are the ways Masonry's openly publicized virtues are outweighed by its hidden vices. By diverting men from the best, Masonry's good selling points become morally twisted, egregiously erroneous, thoroughly bad, grievously misleading and, in the end, fatally false, dark evils that, if followed, will lead straight to perdition.

#2 - How Could So Many Great Men Be So Wrong?

We have given above a very impressive list of this world's great men who chose to join the Masonic lodge. They saw it as good, wise, and upright. I am not challenging their personal accomplishments, their worldly greatness, or their worldly wisdom. These are commendable. But I am challenging their spiritual and moral judgment concerning Freemasonry's biblicality, claims, and teachings. On this issue, they were profoundly wrong. But how could so many of this world's great men be so wrong?

Concisely, the answer is *worldly greatness* is not *spiritual greatness*. National or international acclaim is not equal to biblical fame. This unredeemed world's powerful and famous men and women do not share the same standing before God as redeemed men and women who have attained spiritual greatness (see Hebrews 11:4-40).

Worldly men live their lives by human reason and worldly standards. They are not guided by God's will, Word, Spirit, calling, or plan. Some want to do good, others seek excellence, or to help their people, or achieve great things in this present fallen social order. All of this is humanly commendable. But to a man they are *not* focused on pleasing God and thus receiving His approval.

Godly men also employ the reasoning God has given them, but they put divine reasoning first and their reasoning second (see Proverbs 3:5-6). They also live by not worldly but biblical standards. And their undergirding and overarching purpose in life is clear and focused: to please God. Consequently, when making life decisions, they do so from an entirely different perspective. They are spiritually minded (or biblically minded, since the Bible is inspired by the Spirit, 2 Timothy 3:16-17). Unlike this world's great men, spiritually great men live not by their own wisdom or this world's standards but by faith in God, the superior wisdom and standards of

His Word, and His Spirit's unerring guidance, all to please Him.

So, these two kinds of "great men" simply do not think alike (see Romans 8:5). One lives by the thought patterns of this world and is acclaimed and rewarded by his public for so doing, because worldly minded men always approve of other worldly-minded men, especially when they are visibly successful. The other seeks Christ's approval alone and lives by biblical thought patterns, with one goal in mind: hearing His "well done" when they finish the race He has set before them (Matthew 25:21, 23).

Therefore, the greatest human achievements on the highest national or international stage offer no proof that one is correct on spiritual or moral issues in God's eyes. Few, if any, who make this world's "who's who" listings will also be included in God's final hall of fame. Secular history and Hebrews 11 speak of two entirely different types of people and greatness. One greatness is temporal; the other is eternal. One greatness appeals to the first Adam's children; the other appeals to the last Adam's children. One man's goals are in this world only; the other's goals lay in the next world. One man lives for personal glory; the other lives for Christ's glory. One man seeks to build his own kingdom of popularity, influence, or power; the other lives only to enlarge, improve, and establish Jesus' kingdom. And there is something else to consider.

Some of this world's great men, while cultivating public images of righteousness and selfless interest in others' welfare, are in private forging morally corrupt characters. As a result, sin blinds their moral vision. These "great" ones, whatever their worldly achievements, are easily deceived in spiritual and moral issues. Thus, their decisions on issues of spirituality and morality will be vastly different from the decisions of men with a spiritual viewpoint and moral lifestyle. To put it differently, an unsaved worldly man of high standing may think something evil (e.g., abortion) is righteous while a saved, obedient, spiritually minded Christian will easily recognize it is wrong. In our context, the once-born worldly man may be very impressed with Masonry's good works and great men, while twice-born spiritually minded Christians will see through them and turn away.

Yes, I am saying what you are thinking. America's great founding fathers, the great George Washington, our great Presidents, movie stars, and influential people named earlier were tragically wrong in one decision: their choice to become Masons. They may have made many wonderful decisions in other issues and thus merit honor in this world. But Christ will never honor them for joining the lodge. Need more examples of great men erring greatly?

Martin Luther stood alone in 1517 after long biblical study and prayerful soul searching led him to bravely denounce the heresies and sins of the all-powerful medieval Roman Catholic Church. For this he was brought to trial. After hearing Luther defend his positions at the Diet of Worms (1521), the Holy Roman Emperor, Charles V, concluded, "A single friar (monk) who goes counter to all Christianity for a thousand years must be wrong."[5] But the great emperor was wrong and the humble friar right. In the issue at hand—the biblicality of the church's teachings and practices—Luther's 95 theses[6] were valid and a thousand years of papal teaching invalid. Want more examples?

Ancient Israel's and Judah's kings were great, larger than life, seemingly infallible in the people's eyes. But consider these kings' choices. King Jeroboam built idol shrines in Israel. King Ahab and Queen Jezebel filled the whole land with Baal worship. King Ahaz of Judah boarded up the temple in Jerusalem and forbade the worship of Yahweh. Meanwhile the people assumed their kings' choices were spiritually and morally right. But just the opposite was true. The great kings' decisions were tragically ungodly and brought not blessing but judgment! The prophets pointed this out, but the people could not bring themselves to believe that their kings, the great leaders they respected so much, had erred. So *they* erred. And together, errant kings and people, went into captivity.

A few centuries later, the Pharisees arose. These righteous-looking, pious-acting Jewish religious leaders did many good works, but with bad motives: to be "seen by men" (Matthew 6:1-2, 5, 16). The people were very impressed with the Pharisees' works. They considered

---

5. Christianity Today, "Luther's Political Nemesis: Charles V (1500-1558)," by Paul Thigpen, see: https://www.christianitytoday.com/1992/04/luthers-political-nemesis/ (accessed 9/12/2024).

6. These 95 "theses" were descriptions of Roman Catholic errors which Luther posted to the door of the church in Wittenburg, Germany to call for a public debate.

them great leaders and assumed all their opinions were correct. After all, they were experts in Bible (Torah) knowledge. But Jesus didn't share the public's view. According to Him, the Pharisees, though seemingly great in righteousness, were actually great sinners. Their religious pride blinded them, leaving them in spiritual darkness, lost, and far from God. They confirmed Jesus' opinion by denouncing Him as a crazy, demonic, false Messiah and insurrectionist. He in turn denounced them as "blind," "hypocrites," and "fools" bound for hell for diligently preventing others from entering God's kingdom (Matthew 23:13-33). Which brings us to our spiritual and moral decision.

Whose side will we choose in this issue of Freemasonry, God's or man's? Will we settle for the good or choose the best? Will we accept a counterfeit or reject it in favor of the genuine? Will great men or biblical truth carry more weight in our minds? Freemasonry's good deeds or Christ's good work? Freemasonry's gospel or God's? Our answer will decide whether we see through Freemasonry's façade or are deceived by it.

Chapter Five

LOOKING FORWARD: OUR COURSE OF ACTION

HAVING EXAMINED Freemasonry's past, present, heresies, and façade, we have only one task remaining to complete our study. But it is a crucial one. Liberating knowledge liberates only when acted upon. The knowledge you have learned calls you to ministerial action, to do what you can to reveal Freemasonry's dark, deadly heresies to men ensnared in or considering it. And to women, girls, and young men also, since, as noted, everything true of Freemasonry is also true of its associate organizations, Eastern Star (for women and men), Rainbow (for girls), and DeMolay (for young men). Since this exposé has presented God's Word, you now know His will or mind on this issue. So, you should ask not *if* you should take action but *how*. This chapter offers practical answers. Let us now review Freemasonry's dark spiritual covering, the apostle Paul's scriptural orders, and recommended courses of action.

FREEMASONRY'S DARK SPIRITUAL COVERING

Born-again Christians are divinely protected by an impenetrable spiritual covering of Christ's atoning blood, a "hedge" of angelic protection (Job 1:10; Psalm 91:10-12), and the "whole armor of God" the apostle Paul described in detail in Ephesians 6:10-18. Wonderful as it is, this divine covering may be penetrated. By swearing loyalty to the dark, unbiblical, satanically authored teachings of Freemasonry, a Christian compromises his undivided allegiance to Christ and His truth. This creates two serious problems that last as long as he remains compromised.

First, it brings the compromised Christian under a covering of spiritual darkness, Satan's "covering cast over all people" and "veil that is spread over all nations" (Isaiah 25:7). This covering by the demonic "rulers of the darkness of this world" (Ephesians 6:12) blocks the true "light"—insight into biblical truth, God's approving favor, the Holy Spirit's guidance, and spiritual discernment—from shining into the Christian's mind as long as he persists in his compromise.

This dark covering leaves him unable to receive a full blessing from reading and studying God's Word. It deprives him of the blessings, joys, and answers to prayer that come when we enjoy God's smile of approval. It makes it difficult, if not impossible, for him to hear God's still, small voice showing him which way to take at crucial crossroads. And it leaves him unable to clearly see God's hand, or Satan's subtle temptations and traps, in his life.

Second, it creates a gap in his divine protection. And know this: though evil, Satan remains an excellent spiritual archer. Given even a small gap, he may inflict serious harm with his "fiery darts" (Ephesians 6:16)—costly adversities, bitter conflicts, lost opportunities, devastating failures, or bitter sorrows—which never would have hit their marks if the Christian had remained uncompromised. In other words, compromised Christians "give place to the devil" (Ephesians 4:26), or give him a spiritual "advantage" over them (2 Corinthians 2:11), so he may harm them in ways he could not have done otherwise. Why?

They are walking in darkness, not light. They are presently under Satan's authority, not Christ's. They are being led by malevolent demons, not the benevolent Holy Spirit. They are in danger, not safety. They are in spiritual captivity, not Christian liberty. And what is worse, deceived, they believe all is well!

Ironically, Freemasonry's name is itself a lie: instead of setting *Free*-masons "free," its core heresies shackle them with spiritual chains, leaving them and their families spiritual captives subject to varying degrees of harmful Satanic influence. Why? Fathers are the spiritual heads and priests of their families. When they give Satan a chance to harm them, they also endanger their wives and children, who are under their spiritual coverings.

For example, tragedy struck Jacob's household when he deferred fully obeying God's call to Bethel (Genesis 31:13). His disobedience compromised his household's divine protection, leaving a gap in his spiritual armor. As a result, his daughter, Dinah, was raped and his sons rashly took revenge by killing all the men of Shechem (Genesis 34:1-31). It was the lowest moment in Jacob's life. But the Shechem tragedy would never have happened if Jacob had returned straight to Bethel as commanded, instead of stopping short at Succoth (and Shalem) and remaining there, out of God's perfect will and protection, for perhaps several years (Genesis 33:17-20).[1] Spiritual compromise cost him dearly. If this seems harsh, let me remind you of two tall truths.

First, God considers partial obedience *rebellion*. Why? We obeyed part of His request, but rebelled against the rest (see 1 Samuel 15:1-23). To rebel brings us back temporarily under the authority of the arch rebel, Satan, and His covering of darkness previously described. Second, as long as we walk closely with God in this godless world, we remain in a fierce, relentless, deadly spiritual war with Satan's dark, demonic forces. They are militantly committed to doing anything they can to deceive, harm, or kill us. So, it is vital that we maintain full personal obedience and full divine protection. Not doing so is too dangerous.

What happens if a Christian, knowing the Masons' dark deceptions and heresies, compromises his walk with Christ by joining them? I cannot tell. No one can tell. But this is sure: he is recklessly exposing his life and his household to Satan's deceptions, traps, and assaults.

The Apostle Paul's Scriptural Orders

The ever-zealous apostle Paul exposed or denounced

---

[1]. When discouraged and in temporary unbelief, David and his men left Israel without God's authorization and lived sixteen months in their enemy's territory (1 Samuel 27:1-7), a similar breach of divine protection occurred (30:1-2). The Ziklag tragedy would not have happened if David had remained obediently in Israel, despite his ongoing difficulties there.

numerous heretics, sects, and secret societies during his ministry, most prominently the Judaizers and Gnostics. With these dark teachings and groups in mind, Paul issued these stark apostolic orders to Christians:

> *Have no fellowship* with the unfruitful works of darkness, but rather *reprove them*.
> —EPHESIANS 5:11

> Let us, therefore, *cast off the works of darkness*, and let us put on [again] the [full] armor of light.
> —ROMANS 13:12

> What fellowship has light with darkness? What accord has Christ with Belial? ... Therefore *go out* from their midst, and *be separate* from them, says the Lord ...
> —2 CORINTHIANS 6:14-15, 17, ESV

With Paul's wise and authoritative instructions in mind, consider these recommended biblical courses of action. They will help you "work out" the knowledge this exposé has "worked into" you (Philippians 2:12-14).

RECOMMENDED COURSES OF ACTION

For Masons

If you are a Christian, or non-Christian, entangled in Freemasonry, Eastern Star, Rainbow, or DeMolay, there is only one acceptable response to Paul's wise apostolic orders: obey them! In his own words—inspired, infallible, biblical directives—the great heresy hunter has laid out his recommended courses of action:

- "CAST OFF THE WORKS OF DARKNESS!" – Throw off

everything Masonic. Renounce your Masonic degree rituals. Renounce your Masonic oaths. Renounce all Masonic teachings. Throw away your Masonic Bibles, books, clothes, hats, gloves, and anything else that entered your life when you entered the lodge.

- "Go out from their midst!" – Leave the company of your Masonic lodge brothers. Abandon the Masonic temple. Never return to Masonic meetings or events for any reason.

- "Have no fellowship!" – Do not attempt to restore fellowship with your former Masonic brothers. And do not accept their attempts to reconnect with you. Unless, of course, they are also ready to leave the lodge.

- "Be ye separate!" – Once you have made a clean break, maintain it. Live the rest of your life separated from everything Masonic. Never again support Masonic or Shriners' charities or other good works. (There are plenty of other charities to give to that have no dark spiritual strings attached.)

After you obey Paul's apostolic orders, Satan will quickly attempt to reassert his dominion over you through your former Masonic associates. Some Masons will angrily reject, criticize, and slander you by misrepresenting your reasons for leaving the lodge. Or they may go further, vengefully trying to make you lose friends, business, employment, promotions, or other opportunities to prosper. Other Masons will try the opposite strategy. They will remain friendly and try to stay in touch, hoping at some point to woo you back into the fraternity. Your resoluteness will remain firm if you remember every truth presented in this book remains true. Time cannot change biblical truth.

Satan will also assault you through your own thoughts. You will find yourself anxiously rethinking your decision-making process. Perhaps you were extreme and acted rashly in leaving the lodge? Or maybe you were being "super spiritual" and were moved by religious pride? Or you were being callous and selfish? You did not stop to think how you would hurt your former Masonic brothers' feelings. Or you may catch yourself reminiscing, remembering the good times, and wishing you could enjoy their fellowship again. Satan will remind you of family members who were Masons before you and accuse you of disrespecting them or thinking you are better than them because you have abandoned the lodge and they did not. In these and many other ways, the deceiver will try to get you to doubt God's Word, minimize the danger of Masonic heresies, and maximize the likelihood that you have made an incorrect decision.

During this post-decision onslaught, remember that, whatever the enemy's methods, his objective is always the same: to move you from your biblical stance! So, keep your loyalties firmly with God's Word. Banish all regret. Be single-minded, unyielding, intrepid. It is important that you make no apologies and feel no shame for your actions. Why? You have honored God by believing biblical truth and obeying apostolic orders. For this, your heavenly Father will honor you, as He promised: "Them that honor me I will honor" (1 Samuel 2:30). He is firmly on your side because you have firmly taken His side. To offer apologies or nurse regret would imply you have retracted your decision. This undermines the moral value of the correct stand you have made and evinces a desire to please yourself or your former Masonic associates more than your heavenly Father. If continued, make no mistake, this will lead you to reverse yourself, rejoin the lodge, restore Satan's dark covering over you and your family, and lose the reward you would have had for obeying Christ wholeheartedly, even when it meant suffering rejection (2 John 8).

And, once free, endeavor to free others. When former Masons ask the reason for your actions, share with them all the biblical insights you have learned from this exposé. Or, in Paul's parlance, "reprove them" with God's truth spoken in God's love. Remember, you are always acting in God's love when you tell people the truth about the falsehoods or sins that are binding them in spiritual darkness, especially when you realize they may reject you for it. Then intercede daily for God to graciously open the eyes of: your former Masonic brothers, especially those with whom you have shared these truths who are still in the Craft; Masons in other lodges in your area; women, young men, and girls in associate Masonic organizations; and anyone you know who is considering becoming a Mason.

For Non-Masons

If you are not a Freemason, here are some things you can do to help minister deliverance to men who are Freemasons and keep others considering Freemasonry from going into spiritual bondage:

- DO NOT JOIN THE MASONS! Don't seek membership in the lodge because wealthy or influential men, fellow professionals, coworkers, or others you know or do business with are Masons. Don't be drawn in by false loyalty to family members who are or were Masons: brothers, fathers, uncles, grandfathers, great-grandfathers. Perhaps they did not know the key facts in this exposé when they chose to become Masons. Don't let their decisions determine yours. Let God's Word be your final authority and put eternal truth before family loyalties. Seize your opportunity to become a bondage breaker! Boldy be the first in your family to reject Masonry and live free from its dark covering. Set a new, godly example for your sons, nephews, grandsons, and great-grandsons to follow.

- PRAY FOR EVERY MASON IN YOUR CIRCLE OF CONTACTS. Persistent, Spirit-filled intercession is powerful: "The earnest prayer of a righteous person has great power and produces wonderful results" (James 5:16, NLT). It will minimize the harmful effects of Satan's dark covering over Masons and their families, and incline their minds to question their Masonic oaths and teachings, and eventually leave the lodge.

- TESTIFY AGAINST THE LODGE AND FOR THE TRUTH. Since Christ has called you to be His "witness" (Acts 1:8), every time God opens a door, testify! Tell whoever will listen what you have learned about the Craft's dark spiritual alignment and the dangers it poses for Masons and their families. And when, to defend the lodge, Masons boast on their good works and great men, acknowledge they are correct. Then explain that good works cannot negate damning heresies,[2] and worldly men, however great, do not always make correct spiritual and moral decisions.

- SHARE THIS BOOK WITH YOUR PASTOR. Many honorable pastors are uninformed on this subject. But, once informed, they will not only take to heart the insights you have just studied but also take action. Remember, when you reach a pastor, you reach a church, and when you reach a church, you reach many families.

- SHARE THIS BOOK OR ITS CONTENTS WITH YOUR FRIENDS. Serious, "remnant" Christians in your church, Bible study, prayer group, men's (or women's) fellowship, or missionary group will be glad to discover these truths. To your surprise, you may discover some are Masons but, when corrected, will repent. Your other friends will share these truths with practicing or prospective Masons in their circles of influence.

- IF YOU ARE A PASTOR OR TEACHER, SPEAK ON THIS SUBJECT. Make Masonry the subject of your next sermon, or teaching series. Also, share it whenever counseling Christian Masons or other inquirers. Truth always liberates humble Christians, many of whom are uninformed, have wrong impressions,

---

2. A religion's good works do not prove its teachings are good (true, valid). The Church of Jesus Christ of Latter-Day Saints (Mormon Church), The Watchtower Society (Jehovah's Witnesses), The Church of Christ, Scientist (Christian Science), The Seventh-Day Adventist Church, The Roman Catholic Church—all these and other cults, pseudo-churches, apostate churches, and false religions do unquestionably good works. But their core salvific doctrines, if believed, lead people to hell rather than heaven.

or have been falsely informed about the lodge. Confronting Masons and the demonic forces influencing them will require courage. You will certainly be rejected by some Masons for exposing their organization's dark heresies. Others, however, will receive your message, thank you, and promptly exit the lodge. But more importantly, God will be pleased and compensate you and the church you pastor for any losses incurred.

- IF YOU ARE IN CHRISTIAN MEDIA, BROADCAST THIS NEWS. Schedule a program, podcast, or interview on Masonry soon so your listeners can receive this vital information. Who knows, your broadcast may liberate a father, a family, or an entire lodge full of formerly uninformed or misinformed Christian Masons. They may then inform a key pastor, denominational leader, editor, Internet influencer, or other person with a large following who may spread this knowledge even farther.[3]

---

3. Two very influential nineteenth-century minsters, Dwight L. Moody and Charles G. Finney, spoke out unambiguously against Freemasonry. I offer Finney's views in the Appendix. Moody stated: "I do not see how any Christian, most of all a Christian minister, can go into these lodges with unbelievers. They say they can have more influence for good, but I say they can have more influence for good by staying out of them and then reproving their evil deeds. You can never reform anything by unequally yoking yourself with ungodly men. True reformers separate themselves from the world. But, some say to me, if you talk that way you will drive all the members of secret societies out of your meetings and out of your churches. But what if I did? Better men will take their places. Give them the truth anyway and if they would rather leave their churches than their lodges, the sooner they get out of the churches the better. I would rather have ten members who are separated from the world that a thousand such members. Come out from the lodge. Better one with God than a thousand without Him. We must walk with God

We have now reached the end of our research. In summation, while not executing an exhaustive study, we have pursued a thorough one. All pertinent facts have been presented. With honesty and without ulterior motives. As stated in the Introduction, I hold no grudge against any Mason. This is a doctrinal, not a personal, polemic. I love Masons as much as anyone else and want to see them all freed by the truth. Nor have I twisted any facts to try to make my arguments more convincing while secretly aware of other facts that would disprove them.

Reviewing our research, we have looked back—to gain an accurate perspective of Freemasonry's origins. We have looked in—to examine its current working parts, the common experiences shared by Masons today. We have looked deeper—to uncover Freemasonry's cleverly disguised and vigorously denied core heresies, and found them to be dark, deceptive and, if believed, damning. We have looked through—penetrating Freemasonry's false façade of good works and great men, and found it misleading. And we have looked forward—presenting biblical recommended courses of action, from no less an authority than the apostle Paul, and describing practically how to implement them.

My desire, and prayer, for you is simple: that you heed this exposé and take its advice. If you are a Christian, may I propose a prayer of renunciation?

---

and if only one or two go with us, it is all right. Do not let down the standard to suit men who love their secret lodges." See: http://www.ephesians5-11.org/finmood.htm (accessed 9/17/2024).

"Heavenly Father, having received the biblical correction inscribed in this book, I fully and willingly renounce everything Masonic: my blood oaths, my degree teachings, Masonry's false gospel, its false god, and every false Masonic myth and doctrine. I ask that You forgive me for submitting to Masonry's lies, cleanse me by Jesus' blood, and receive me back into full fellowship with You—the only true divine Light of this world and my life. Amen!"

And as for this book, I pray:

"Heavenly Father, may this small book have a large ministry. May Your Holy Spirit's awesome power flow through it, delivering many Masons and keeping many others from Masonic bondage. For the sake of Your mercy. For the honor of Christ. For the preparation of His bride, the church, for His impending return. Amen!"

APPENDIX

MORGAN, FINNEY, AND REVIVAL

AUTHOR'S NOTE: This report of American Freemasonry's lowest hour, the Morgan scandal, in no way implies Masons today would conspire to murder. But honesty requires I note the conspirators, while pushed beyond reason, were merely acting out the reasonable conclusion of their Masonic blood oaths. Perhaps Masons will reconsider and eliminate all such oaths.

NO EXPOSÉ OF FREEMASONRY would be complete without describing the infamous William Morgan affair of 1826. Called by some the "Watergate" of the nineteenth century, its jolting of America cannot be overstated. We will review the central facts and then show how this New York scandal commanded the attention of one of America's most famous evangelists and helped spark a great awakening.

Captain William Morgan was a typical nineteenth-century American citizen. A bricklaying stone worker and veteran of the War of 1812, after which he attained (or claimed) the rank of captain, Morgan settled in Batavia, New York, where he became a Mason. Completing the first three (Blue Lodge) degrees, he became a Master Mason and attended lodge meetings faithfully for thirty years. He became disillusioned with his Masonic experience, however, when he saw the unquestioned power and questionable means of his Masonic brothers in running local politics and government. Determined to right his soul by exposing Masonry's wrongs, Morgan acquired a like-minded publisher, David Miller, and proceeded to write a tell-all book bringing to light the Craft's dark secrets and practices. By writing *Illustrations of Masonry, by One of The Fraternity Who Has Devoted Thirty Years to The Subject*,[1] Morgan was breaking the solemn Masonic blood oath he took promising to never divulge the Craft's precious secrets.

Panicky at the thought of their secrets becoming known, and infuriated at Morgan for his oath-breaking, his Masonic brothers first deliberated and then acted. Initially, they harassed him and his publisher. They filed unfounded lawsuits against Miller, attacked his publishing office, and even set fire to it, though with little actual damage. Determined, Morgan and Miller didn't yield. Neither did the Masons! Using their heavy influence with the local courts and law enforcement, the Masons trumped-up three separate false charges against Morgan for alleged petty crimes, the last landing him in jail. Then, on the night of September 11, 1826, after paying Morgan's bail without his knowledge or consent, three Masons hastily abducted him.[2]

---

1. Internet Archive Online, https://archive.org/details/illustrationsofm00morg/page/12/mode/2up?view=theater (accessed 9/18/2024).

2. A local Mason, Samuel D. Green, wrote a memoir, *The Broken Seal*, exposing the Morgan abduction and murder plot. He concluded that, based on lodge proceedings and conversations he witnessed after Morgan's abduction, Morgan's captors were not hot-headed young Masons acting in spontaneous passion, but rather the lodge's most distinguished, Masonically educated leaders carrying out a carefully reasoned plot. "These men, who were the leaders in this plot against Morgan and Miller, were men of standing and character. They were at the time holding the most important offices in church and state … Everything had been considered and determined upon by the very highest authorities in the Masonic councils." See: Smithsonian Maga-

As they shoved him into a waiting carriage, he reportedly shouted, "Murder!" Obviously, he feared the worst. And promptly, they did the worst.

Nearly twenty years later, in 1848, a death-bed confession by Henry L. Valance, one of Morgan's abductors, revealed what actually happened. Morgan's three Masonic captors took him during the night by boat into the swift Niagara river and, with Morgan's body heavily weighted, Valance pushed him overboard.[3] Morgan was never again seen. He left behind a wife and two children.

Four Masons charged with doing away with Morgan—Loton Lawson, Eli Bruce, Col. Edward Sawyer, Nicholas G. Chesebro—were put on trial in January 1827.[4] Due to powerful local Masonic influence, they were convicted not of conspiracy to commit murder but simply of "forcibly moving Morgan from one place to another against his will," since this was all that could be legally proven. (Valance had not yet confessed.) They served light sentences ranging from one month to two

---

zine Online, "The Masonic Murder that Inspired the First Third Party in American Politics," by Colin Dickey, https://www.smithsonianmag.com/history/the-masonic-murder-that-inspired-the-us-first-third-party-180982495/ (accessed 9/18/2024).

3. Green, Samuel D., *The Broken Seal: Or Personal Reminiscences of the Morgan Abduction and Murder* (Classic Reprint), (London, GB; Forgotten Books), 2018, 296-299.

4. The History Channel Online, "One Man Exposed the Secrets of Freemasons. His Disappearance Led to Their Downfall," by Martin Stezano, see: https://www.history.com/news/freemason-secrets-revealed (accessed 9/18/2024).

years. With neither Morgan nor his corpse ever being found, it seemed obvious to the average person, that the Masons had gotten away with murder. The public was outraged.

Sensing this, the Masons quickly devised dubious cover stories to quell the furor. Some said Morgan was merely paid to leave the country and not return. Others said he traveled to the Caymen Islands and was later reunited with his wife and children there. Still others said they had seen him living under an assumed name. Privately, many Masons felt Morgan got what he deserved: he broke his most solemn oath and he most solemnly paid for it! The public vigorously disagreed and rejected out of hand the implausible Masonic defenses.

As the news of Morgan's abduction spread, anti-Masonic sentiment swept the nation. The Masonic lodges, which were very numerous and powerful in America at the time, suffered steady attrition over the ensuing years until reduced to a mere shadow of their formerly potent selves.

Many ministers began speaking out against Masonic heresies. Soon American Christians acted decisively against everything Masonic. Many churches refused Communion to Masons. Others presented their Masonic members with an ultimatum: leave the lodge or the church! Among the ministers speaking out was the famous evangelist, pastor, and scholar, Charles G. Finney, who had been a Master Mason before seeing the light and exiting the Masonic darkness.

In Finney's exhaustive exposé, *The Character, Claims,*

and Practical Workings of Freemasonry,[5] the former lawyer's sweeping indictment made numerous charges with prosecutorial precision: the lodge was a false religion, its oaths were unbiblical, its members were sworn to persecute defecting Masons, its claims to antiquity were false, its professed benevolence is a sham, it was guilty of numerous other wrongs, and no credible Masonic defense had been presented. Case closed!

So strong were the public's anti-Masonic sentiments throughout the land that an official "Anti-Mason Party" was formed. It even nominated a candidate, William Wirt, for the Presidency, who ran against Andrew Jackson and Henry Clay. He lost, but the anti-Masonic wave rolled on.

During this period of prevailing anti-Masonic sentiments, the third phase[6] of the Second Great Awakening ignited in New York state in 1825, sparked by Finney's new, dynamic evangelistic methods. Through the preaching of Finney and others, many thousands across America gave their lives to Jesus during this period (c. 1826-1835) and several cities in New York where Finney's revival meetings occurred were dramatically impacted.[7] What part anti-Masonic sentiments had

---

5. Finney, Charles G., *The Character, Claims, and Practical Workings of Freemasonry*, (Edinburgh, Scotland; CrossReach Publications), 2022.

6. The first and second phases of the Second Great Awakening are generally accepted as occurring from 1795 to 1810 and 1810 to 1825. The third occurred from 1825 to 1835 (or 1840).

7. Some of these were Utica, Troy, Rome, Auburn, Buffalo, New York City, and especially, Rochester. Western New York became known as the "burned-over district." This was "a reference to the fact that the

in this revival is impossible to specify, but it is equally impossible to deny it played a large role. Masonic lodges were significantly impacted by the Awakening. Thousands of Masons, still reeling from shame over the William Morgan affair, renounced their Masonic vows, left the lodge, received Jesus as their Lord and Savior, and joined Christian churches.

Finney estimated that of the approximately 50,000 Masons in America in 1826, some 45,000 turned from the Masons to the Messiah. Even if Finney's figures, which at best would have been difficult to verify, are exaggerated, it is nevertheless true thousands of Masons left the Craft for the Christ.

So, we conclude, there was a spiritual link between Morgan, Finney, and revival. God, as He always does, turned a great evil into a greater good. What even greater good might He do today, on the eve of Christ's Second Coming, if there was another mass exodus from the lodge to the Lord?

---

area had experienced so much religious enthusiasm—from revivals and new religions, to cults and spiritualism—that the district had been scorched." See: https://www.christianitytoday.com/1988/10/charles-grandison-finney-father-of-american-revivalism/ (accessed 9/19/2024).

BIBLIOGRAPHY

In preparing this book, I researched or used information from the following books and websites:

Books

Carlson, Ron, Decker, Ed. *Fast Facts on False Teachings.* Eugene, OR: Harvest House Publishers, 1994.

Finney, Charles G. *The Character, Claims, and Practical Workings of Freemasonry.* Edinburg, Scotland: CrossReach Publications, 2022.

Green, Samuel D. *The Broken Seal: Or Personal Reminiscences of the Morgan Abduction and Murder.* Classic Reprint. London, GB: Forgotten Books, 2018.

Keener, Craig S., Walton, John H. *NIV Cultural Backgrounds Study Bible.* Grand Rapids, MI: Zondervan, 2016.

Mackey, Albert G. *The Symbolism of Freemasonry.* New York, NY: Clark and Maynard, 1882.

Morgan, William. *Illustrations of Masonry, by One of The Fraternity Who Has Devoted Thirty Years to The Subject.* Charleston, SC: Create Space Independent Publishing / Kindle Direct Publishing, 2012.

Newton, Joseph Ford. *The Builders.* Richmond, VA: Macoy Publishing, 1979.

Pike, Albert. *Morals and Dogmas.* Ottawa, ON: East India Publishing, 2022.

Strong, J. *A Concise Dictionary of the Words in the Greek Testament and The Hebrew Bible.* Bellingham, WA: Logos Bible Software, 2009.

The Holy Bible, Heirloom Family Edition. Wichita, KS: Heirloom Bible Publishers, 1988.

The Holy Bible, Master Mason Edition. Wichita, KS: Heirloom Bible Publishers, 1991.

Websites

https://www.adventist.org – The official website of the Seventh Day Adventist Church.

https://www.ancient-origins.net – The official website of Ancient Origins: Unraveling the Mysteries of the Past, whose aim is "to inspire open-minded learning about our past for the betterment of our future through the sharing of research, education, and knowledge."

https://archive.org – Internet Archive is a non-profit library of millions of free books, movies, software, music, websites, and more.

https://www.businessinsider.in - The official website of Business Insider India Online Magazine. BI India is "the Indian edition of Business Insider (BI) - the fastest growing business news website around the globe."

https://www.britannica.com – The official website of Encyclopedia Britannica. "For more than 250 years, Britannica has kindled the spark of curiosity with stories of discoveries, people and events that changed the world."

https://www.charlesgfinney.com – The Charles G. Finney Website, hosting the complete works of Charles G. Finney, unchanged and unabridged.

https://www.christianitytoday.com – The official website of Christianity Today magazine and ministry. "Christianity Today is a voice for the church that shapes the evangelical conversation, brings important issues to the forefront, and challenges Christians to love and serve the overlooked."

http://www.ephesians5-11.org – The official website of Ephesians 5:11, a counter-cult ministry which specializes in subversive religious organizations which deny being religions.

https://www.freemason.com – The official website of the Grand Masonic Lodge of Ohio.

https://www.freemasoninformation.com – Freemason Information is an independent voice in the Masonic community featuring Masonic Education, Analysis and News for Freemasons.

https://freemasonrymatters.co.uk – The official website of Freemasonry Matters, which endeavors "to show the collective positive force Freemasonry has on ourselves, communities & Charity."

http://www.freemasonscommunity.life – Freemasons Community is a virtual temple dedicated to exploring the rich traditions, teachings, and symbolism of Freemasonry.

https://www.grandlodge-nc.org – The official website of the Grand Masonic Lodge of North Carolina.

https://www.history.com – The official website of The History Channel Online. "The History Channel, a division of A & E Networks, is the premier destination for historical storytelling … [and] serves as the most trustworthy source of informational entertainment in media.

https://www.ldsliving.com – The official website of LDS Living Magazine. This site, and its magazine, give expression to what it means to live as a member of The Church of Jesus Christ of Latter-day Saints.

Bibliography

https://dictionary.cambridge.org – Cambridge Dictionaries Online is an official website of the Cambridge University Press, which has been publishing dictionaries for learners of English since 1995.

https://masonicfind.com – The official website of MasonicFind, which, since 2013, has been dedicated to teaching members and non-members about Freemasonry.

https://masonicvibe.com - The official website of Masonic Vibe, which is "building the lodge for the future century by inspiring the younger generation."

http://mason33.org – The official website of the Grand Masonic Lodge of Georgia.

https://www.shrinersinternational.org – The official website of Shriners International.

https://www.smithsonianmag.com – The official website of the Smithsonian Magazine, which places a Smithsonian lens on the world, looking at the topics and subject matters researched, studied and exhibited by the Smithsonian Institution—science, history, art, popular culture and innovation.

https://www.themasonslady.com – The Mason's Lady blog, which serves as a guidebook to answer questions for women whose husbands or friends are, or who are considering becoming, Freemasons.

https://www.thesquaremagazine.com – The official website of The Square magazine, which, published independently of all Grand Lodges, brings you in-depth and thought-provoking articles on all aspects of Freemasonry written by the leading Masonic writers from around the world.

https://www.tms.edu – The official website of The Master's Seminary. Since 1986, The Master's Seminary and Grace Community Church have partnered together to train the future generation of faithful pastor-theologians.

http://web.archive.org – The official website of The Internet Archive Wayback Machine, which "enables you to capture, manage and search collections of digital content without any technical expertise or hosting facilities."

https://www.Wikipedia.org – The official website of Wikipedia, the free online encyclopedia hosted by the Wikimedia Foundation, a non-profit organization that also hosts a range of other projects.

OTHER BOOKS BY THE AUTHOR

Walking in His Ways

Walking on Water

RevelationNotes: An Inspirational Commentary on the Book of Revelation

The Second Coming of Christ: His Appearing, His Return, Our Preparation

The Tribulation Story: A Story You Need to Read About A Time You Need to Escape

The Day of The Lord Commentary: Interpreting Old Testament End-Times Prophecy

DanielNotes: An Inspirational Commentary on the Book of Daniel

ColossianNotes: An Inspirational Commentary on Paul's Epistle to the Colossians

PhilippianNotes: An Inspirational Commentary on Paul's Epistle to the Philippians

Overcoming Adversity: Life-Changing Biblical Insights on Christian Difficulties

Gold Tried in the Fire: Tested Truths for Trying Times

Precious Pearls from The Proverbs

Word Portraits: Five Illustrations of the Mature Christian

Not by Bread Alone: Daily Devotions for Disciples, Volume One

Sweeter Than Honey: Daily Devotions for Disciples, Volume Two

Water from the Rock: Daily Devotions for Disciples, Volume Three

Key New Testament Passages on Divorce and Remarriage

ABOUT THE AUTHOR

Greg Hinnant, D.D., is a Bible expositor, teacher, author, and pastor. His teaching and writing ministries are founded on years of devotional and systematic study of the Bible and Christian history, and have been heavily influenced by the teachings of Oswald Chambers and A. W. Tozer, as well as those of many other Christian scholars, pastors, and leaders.

Greg is a long-standing faculty member and regent of Christian Life School of Theology Global (CLST-Global) and ministers in churches, schools, and conferences.

Dr. Hinnant has published eighteen books in the genres of Christian Living, Devotionals, Biblical Commentary, Polemic Theology, and End-Times Studies, and contributed to the *Spirit Led Woman Bible*. For many years his articles have appeared regularly in Christian periodicals. He releases e-Devotionals, Christian living pieces, audio messages, and "Hinnant Minutes" YouTube videos regularly.

CONTACT INFORMATION:

Greg Hinnant Ministries
P. O. Box 788
High Point, N.C. 27262
Telephone: (336) 882-1645
Email: rghministries@aol.com
Website: greghinnantministries.org
YouTube: Greg Hinnant
Facebook: Greg Hinnant